Handwriting Analysis

A Step by Step Guide to Improve Your Handwriting

(An Illustrated Book on Graphology for Beginners)

Sarah Stewart

Published By **Bella Forst**

Sarah Stewart

Handwriting Analysis: A Step by Step Guide to Improve Your Handwriting (An Illustrated Book on Graphology for Beginners)

ISBN 978-1-77485-507-2

Legal & Disclaimer

The information contained in this ebook is not designed to replace or take the place of any form of medicine or professional medical advice. The information in this ebook has been provided for educational & entertainment purposes only.

The information contained in this book has been compiled from sources deemed reliable, and it is accurate to the best of the Author's knowledge; however, the Author cannot guarantee its accuracy and validity and cannot be held liable for any errors or omissions. Changes are periodically made to this book. You must consult your doctor or get professional medical advice before using any of the suggested remedies, techniques, or information in this book.

Upon using the information contained in this book, you agree to hold harmless the Author from and against any damages, costs, and expenses, including any legal fees potentially resulting from the application of any of the information provided by this guide. This disclaimer applies to any damages or injury caused by the use and application, whether directly or indirectly, of any advice or information presented, whether for breach of contract, tort, negligence, personal injury, criminal intent, or under any other cause of action.

You agree to accept all risks of using the information presented inside this book. You need to consult a professional medical practitioner in order to ensure you are both able and healthy enough to participate in this program.

Table of Contents

Introduction

Have you ever wondered why you go to the doctor and then he hand over an article that includes some medical warnings and requirements for medical tests, however, you're unable to comprehend the information on the document handed to you that is intended for an expert in laboratory science or pharmacist.

Everyone was probably taught to write as children in kindergarten or elementary schools. Regardless how we wrote, our style of writing probably when compared to your current style of writing could have drastically changed The changes you see could be in the size of the writing as well as wavyline, slant spacing, thickness and many other aspects. The changes that subconsciously show appear could be influenced by external factors like our environment or the people with whom we have close proximity with.

This leads us to the realization that one's life experiences as well as their emotional state may have an influence on the writing. The persona of different people plays a part in their writing style. The brain part that is involved in emotional intelligence affects the way we write. Therefore, there is a connection between emotional intelligence and the art of writing.

The emotional intelligence is also a concern for our response to situations, our attitudes toward others and our display of compassion. When we respond to how intelligent an emotionally intelligent person is the writing style of their might change, particularly when a negative situation occurs that can cause anger in the minds of an individual.

The changes in one's mental state can result in changes to one's handwriting. In the end, each person is unique in their way of writing, which is just as individual as our fingerprint print. Even twins born in the same year don't have the identical handwriting. A father and daughter might have similar handwriting styles, but they're not identical. This distinct advantage of the variations in handwriting between individuals allows experts to track and locate suspects in crimes.

The traits mentioned earlier may be a factor in the temperament that is displayed by different people. Giving some insight into the temperament of people, it's widely acknowledged to have four main types of temperament, including melancholy and sanguine as well as that is choleric and phlegmatic. These types of temperaments are further subdivided into more expressive types that are known as the extroverts, and the more reserved ones, referred to as introverts. When it comes to handwriting the introverted or extroverted character of the person who writes the handwriting may be determined from the characteristics related to the two groups of individuals when they write.

The Sanguine and choleric personality or the personality that is known as the extraverted temperament are usually associated with those who tilt towards the right when writing the letters they write as well as melancholy and phlegmatic, which are commonly called the introverted temperament typically are writers who slant their letters to the left as they write.

People who have an extraverted personality tend to be extremely expressive and emotional, with an appreciation for the emotions of other people. The introverted temperament is associated with people who aren't as expressive or emotional, but more rational and analytical.

The book can also help us draw inferences like, an individual's emotional ability, temperament, or personality index of happiness, the typical facial expressions, etc. It is worth noting that the environment influences the persona of an individual, which can have a direct impact on the handwriting of a person. It is widely acknowledged that the character of a mature man is determined by the setting where he grew up.

People who are more bold and more courageous in their outlook appear to reflect that in their writing style This boldness could manifest itself in their bold approach to writing, as will be discussed.

The following information provides more details on handwriting analysis;

Chapter 1: Handwriting Analysis 101

The handwriting of a person is a representation of their psychological state. It's similar to body language . What's within the mind manifests in facial expressions, posture , and actions. Writing is a process that involves your brain (the subconscious) that holds memories. They influence the way documents written appear. Because the subconscious operates on symbols messages from the subconscious get through to how the writer creates his or her penmanship.

Here are a few things that may be found in the written text:

* Hidden secrets
* Past experiences
* Memories
* Emotional development
* Guilt
* Dishonesty
Female or masculine
* Sensitivity
* Potential
* Friendliness
* The nuances of thought
* Ego development
* Energy level
* Refrains and fears

* Self-control
Psychogram

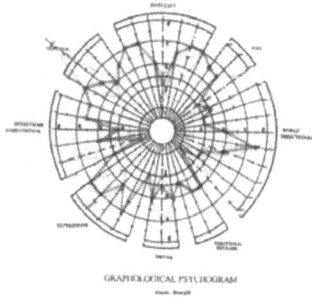

GRAPHOLOGICAL PSYCHOGRAM

The Roman-Staempfli Psychogram can be described as graphology tool used to measure characteristics of the writer's personality. It is circular in shape and divided into quadrants and segments:
* Top: Intellect
* Upper right: ego
* Upper left: control
* Right social
* Left in the direction of inhibitions
Lower right lower right
* Lower left: repressions
* Bottom Drive

The top half of the circle covers the conscious aspects of the person such as the mind, self-control, and the ego.

The lower portion is a part of the unconscious mind, including vitality, emotional release and defenses from the subconscious.

The left part of the circle is what is known as the introverted (self-centered) part that is the persona, for example, controlling and inhibitions.

Right side is an extrovert (people-oriented) side which displays the ego as well as social interactions.

It is helpful to keep a mental picture of the psychogram in mind. This will aid in understanding the way graphology works.

Be aware that there are certain things which aren't easily identified by writing. The most common are:

* Gender (but both femininity and masculinity are exposed)

* Age (but you can determine how you can tell how)

* Handedness (whether the person is right or left handed)

In this regard, it is important to have a basic understanding of the person , including how old they are or gender, as well as which hand is used for writing. These are the things to consider when looking at the penmanship.

This is how the writer's mind is represented on paper:

Paper represents the stage on which the writer performs

Space: The ways spaces are utilized can tell you what the writer's view of the world around him/her.

The writing's movement provides clues about the writer's behavior and actions. The penmanship's movement is three-dimensional.

* Strokes are the name given to these to represent the horizontal (up as well as down) dimension

* Slants can be visible from the vertical (left as well as right) dimension.

* Pressure - These are the levels of text (in both directions)

Forms: The form of the writing material reflect the writer's view of their own self

Strokes: Describe the patterns of the writer's head

Downstrokes: They are the "backbones" of letters. They are created by using thick strokes. They symbolize the portion of the person which is unable to move. Additionally, since they are produced by the hand muscles being contracted they represent the willpower of the writer.

Horizontal strokes: They are made by making gentle outward movements that are akin to the release. Horizontal strokes illustrate how an individual moves and reacts to the things and the environment surrounding him.

Zones: A letter is split into three parts that are the middle, upper, and lower zones. Each zone reveals something about the writer and the way in which these zones are divided gives information about the writer.

* Top the level: thinking, intelligence and imagination.

* Middle: everyday life, socialability and the ego

* Lower: Instincts

Baseline slant: The angle at which the lines written in relation to with the baseline horizontal (printed as printed or unprinted) is a measure of the writer's mood .

* Extreme upward tilt: restlessness, impracticality, joy

* Moderate upward tilt: energy, optimism, ambition

* Horizontal: stability, self-control

* Moderate downward tilt: sadness, pessimism, lethargy
* Extreme downward tilt: depression, hopelessness
Baseline conformity: The method of ensuring that his or her line adheres to the baseline reveals something about their self-control. The baseline is situated in the middle of the upper, middle and the lower zone. It acts as a mediator between the ideals of a person as well as social obligations and desires.
* Lines that are straight but loose demonstrate simplicity and dependability
* Wavy lines indicate mood changes and a lack of carelessness
Straight lines are a sign of rigidity, and the fear of losing control
Slant: The angle of the letters relative towards the vertical lines is what determines the extent of expressiveness and involvement in the social sphere.
Pressure: This is the force that is used to write letters evident in the size and thickness of the text reveals the level of energy used by the writer.
Size The length of the writing shows what the author value his or her personal actions.

* Big Pride, a need to be noticed, extravagant behaviors, exaggeration
* Small: humility focus, independence, the ability to moderate
Spacing: the spacing between elements within the text is a way of determining how the writer places himself or herself within a given situation or in relation to others.
Line space: the space between the writer's thoughts and his/her personal feelings
Spaces between words The space between the creator and other writers
Spaces between letters Show if you like being around others
Between the lines
Wide space: distrust of others, isolation anxiety, isolation, excessive
* Moderate spacing to ensure balance and clarity
A narrow spacing means attachment dependence and confusion
In the form of
• Wide space: open personality, likes to be with others
The spacing is narrow: insecure character, shy, prefers being in a room by itself
Between the words

"Wide spacing: require lots of space from others

The narrow spacing search for companionship

The chapters to follow will examine each of them in greater detail.

Writing Speed

The speed at which the writing is done provides information about the writer's mental and physical capabilities. It's difficult to judge speed if you don't know the way it was written but there are indicators that reveal how fast or slow it was written.

Fast

* Illegible
* Penmanship that flows
* Medium to light pressure
* Left margin grows
* The margin on the right decreases.
* Ovals with well-defined lines
* Short strokes at the beginning
* Strokes come on the right
* Final strokes begin to taper off
* Baseline slightly increases
* Loops have moderate amplitude.
* Loops expand little to the left
* Long T crosses
* T is cross-cut on the left side of the stem
* Stroke-free strokes

* Dots resemble dashes
* Mixed forms
* Forms that are simplified
* Missing details
* Wide
Slow
* School-type penmanship
* Frequent change of direction, breaks in words
* Heavy pressure
* The left margin is reduced
* The margin for the right increases.
* Ovals filled with ink
* Long-ending strokes
* Strokes are finished toward the left
* The final strokes increase
* Final strokes are either blunt or curved
* Dots are round.
* Forms that are consistent
* Elaboration
* Details
* Narrow
Moderately fast
Fast but moderately: confidence, authenticity, honesty, spontaneity and impatience
Fast writing shows confidence and a commitment to communicating the message instead of glossing over formalities and styles.

It also indicates the authenticity and spontaneity. The writer is quick to react. They are quick learners and quick to think. Due to his/her efficiency and speed, he/she might be irritable with those who aren't able to keep up.

Keep in mind that those who usually write slowly might accelerate when they're in a hurry. Review various writing samples to determine the speed at which writers write.

Extremely quick

Very fast, impatience recklessness, carelessness, irritation

The writing speed is extremely fast and difficult to read. The punctuation marks and letters are frequently removed. The t-bars and dots appear created by the form of a jabbing motion. They reflect the writer's recklessness and insanity. Because of his/her strong desire to perform tasks quickly and in a hurry, he/she might not have time to review details and look deeper. Therefore, they tend to be impulsive and insecure. The pressure inside can make him/her angry and hyper-react to even the smallest things.

Slow

Slow: thinks slow and is cautious and careful and doesn't show emotion Self-reliant, self-confident, systematic, and organized

It is when a writer is unable to focus. This is accompanied by self-control, inhibitions, as well as reflection. The person is not a fan of spontaneity and prefers to plan things out in advance. So, he or she won't act or say, or even decide anything until they have considered it carefully. A meticulous and reflective writer excels with tasks which require a lot of focus. But, do not rush him or her as he/she may become stressed under pressure.

Also, you must determine if the writer naturally slows down or is affected by mental or physical factors. Check out similar writing styles to see whether it's consistent.

Extremely slow

Extremely slow mental impairment or anxiety, dishonesty, and depression

Extremely slowing is a indicator for mental decline. If the slowness isn't caused by illness or drugs, the person writing could be deliberately slowing the pace at which he/she is working. It could mean that the writer is trying to conceal something. It could also mean the person is feeling anxious right now.

Examine the writing across the entire page. Slowing down will help the writing appear larger and spaces appear wider.

Average speed

Normal speed: Conventionality Good impulse control

A writer with a regular pace of writing is a person with even temper. He/she isn't too fast or forced to focus. He may process concepts that are new to him, but is not required to take time to study them.

Summary

Speed is a measure of the ability as well as the maturity and spontaneity that the author has. It is best to observe the writer, however you can judge speed by the size of the letters, shape as well as spacing, slant and stroke direction, as well as the writing pressure. Beware of extremely slow writing, as this is an indication that the writer might be hiding somethingor is impaired due to mental illness or an energizing substance.

Rhythm

The rhythm, or the rhythm and the regularity of writing reflect the individual's behavior. It is a reflection of the flow of energy in the individual.

There are two types of handwriting strokes which are curved and linear. Linear strokes are those that go only in one direction and curly strokes can be either centrifugal (moving away in the direction of the central point) as well as centripetal (turning towards from the middle). The method a writer uses to create straight and curved strokes can affect their rhythm.

A writer might have an innate or weak irregular feeling of rhythm.

Strong

* Outward movement
* No sudden changes
* Fluid
* Natural
* Curved
* Sharp turn points at the turning point.
* Complex motions
* Even margins
* Even word spacing
* Good zone balance
* Missing the initial strokes
* Stroke at the end missing

Weak

* Inward movement
* Forms that are unnatural
* Simple motions

* Dragging strokes
* Low pressure
* Large spaces
* Unevenly distributed space
* Margins not observed
* The emphasis is on one area.
* Letters that are narrow or wide
* Stroke with emphasis at the end
* Small letters
* Prominent spaces
Disturbed
* Chopped strokes
* Pressure that is not even
* Changes to writing characteristics (pressure and dimensions, etc.)
* Jerky motions
* Angular letters
* Imbalanced zones
* Text overlay
* Large letters
* Uneven word spacing and margins
* Exaggerations
* Extremely angry
Strong
Writing that is characterized by a the ability to write with a strong rhythm is created by someone who has a balanced personality.
Weak

A low rhythm can be a sign of anxiety or inhibitions. It is possible that the person is having issues in certain aspects of their lives.

Disturbed

The erratic rhythm indicates unreliability as well as instability, inconsistency and inconsistency. It could indicate extreme emotions that are not easily manageable. If you can see them in someone else it is easy to tell the emotions he/she's experiencing. The person is likely to be hypersensitive too.

The writer could also be confused about numerous things. They can change their minds rapidly. The writer may have several thousand things going on in his/her head, and cannot think deeply about anything.

Summary

A rhythm that is strong creates penmanship that is steady and smooth. A weak rhythm can have constant flow but isn't fluid. A rhythm that is unstable and changes between weak and strong. It is possible to determine the type of rhythm is utilized by the features of penmanship. They reveal the writer's energy patterns.

Formulas

Forms and shapes create images of what happens inside the writer's brain.

Overall Form Quality

It is easy to determine the character of a person by observing these characteristics:

Embellished/Ornate letters

When writing appears more complex and artful than the norm it could be a sign of something like formality, vanity, arousal to self-esteem and deceit.

Simplified

Simple penmanship is comprised of simple strokes. It is a sign of maturity, practicality openness, honesty, and transparency.

Not listened to

Neglected writing contains punctuations, strokes and letters. It signifies depression, secretiveness withdrawal, and issues.

Legible

A legitimate penmanship style is one that is meticulous and a clear mind. If it is closely resembling the style of a copybook is also a sign of conventionality.

Illegible

A person who has handwriting that isn't legible might be impatient and careless. It can also refer to fraud. The topic of dishonesty will be covered in a subsequent chapter.

Tangled

Tangled lines indicate an exuberant persona.

Capitals printed on paper

The people who print capitals are thought to be straight people.

A variety of traits are usually attributed to one penmanship attribute. To determine which characteristic is applicable to the individual, look up the other information in the article.

Shapes

The general form of strokes and letters is a sign of a particular type of personality

* Arcade: protects traditional boundaries and boundaries, and is constant

* Garland is open to new ideas as well as other people, flexible

* Angle: determination or intelligence, as well as aggression.

* Thread: quick-mindedness as well as diplomacy, creativity, and a sense of humor

Arcade

The arcade type has arched-like letters and connectors. They have curved tops as well as open bottoms. Writers create these patterns while subconsciously protecting some thing. Penmanship that is arcade-style can be described as secure, reliable and self-reliant. They also have a knack for keeping secrets. On the other hand they are extremely solitary, stubborn and selective of those who aren't to the same social group as they do.

It is the principle that drives the arcade. People with this kind of mindset take their time before taking any action. They take this action to protect themselves as well as others. It is possible that they carry an air of seriousness around them.

Capital letters M and the smaller letters h and n are both examples of arcades. Connectors between the smaller letter s, the letters and w, and another letter could also represent arcades.

Garland

People with garland letters are opposite of arcade people. The letters they write on have an inverted arch that looks like cups. The lower parts of connectors are curving while their tops are open. These characteristics indicate that people who wear garland are open to other people. They are usually kind and compassionate. They tend to put their feelings ahead of rationality.

Garlands are easy to find since they are very prevalent in writing. Find them in the connecting letters in the beginning and at the end of words, as well as anywhere within all three areas.

Angle

An angled design has distinct points. It is typically seen among those who are analytical and curious.

Angles develop when a writer writes fast and is forced to take abrupt changes in the structure that compose the words. Because angles aren't flowing seamlessly into the next letter word, they can cause short gaps. Writers who are comfortable with this type of composition are the ones who routinely take a moment to reflect on things. Some of the qualities that could come from this include control, determination and sharp perception.

To find angles, examine the middlezone alphabet, along with the base along with the highest points of the letters.

Thread

The style of writing depicts the thread-like qualities. It can be seen in writers who are clever creative, imaginative, and flexible. They have a knack for joining different things together to come up with something new, or to come up with a concept. They rarely jump into action immediately, but wait until the right time to start doing things. This is why they're not well-suited for initiating things, but they are able to react well to what is happening already. One of the negative characteristics of people with thread penmanship include that they are deceiving and reckless at times.

There are many kinds of threads:

Thin strokes

It is possible to observe that strokes shrink because less pressure is employed in making strokes. They can be seen among the dots in i's as well as those of the crosses on t's and also between two letters, and at the end of words. If you spot these, the author you're looking at might have these traits: a tendency to hurry things along and be impatient, careless and a lack of desire to finish the job.

The size of letters in words

If the ending letters of the word are less than the letters that begin the word the writer who changes his or her viewpoint to remain calm. The way in which the letters shrink represents the move out of the situation in order to view the entire scene. One can effortlessly shift between different ways of dealing with interpersonal conflicts and issues.

Sinuous strokes

Sinuous strokes can be described as snake-like forms which are the most apparent when writing middle-zone letters. They are made using swift moves. This type of style is indicative of a tendency to ignore problems or obligations.

Wavyline

Wavyline is a blend of various styles. It's performed by people who have the maturity and high levels of intelligence. They are expected to make efficient use of resources and easily adapt to changing situations.

Summary

The quality and form of writing are a reflection of the writer's character. Before you make any decisions make sure to verify the information.

Zones

Handwriting analysis is the process of analyzing handwriting. A text line splits into 3 zones that are the middle, upper and the lower zone. The zones are used as a representation of an individual. It also represents the past, present and the future. The downward and upward movements of writing determine the characteristics of every zone.

Upper: Mind, Spirituality Intellect, goals, conscience, the upper portion of our body the future

Middle: ego, normal emotional, and activity and ego, middle three of our body in the present

Lower: Physicality, fundamental desires, instincts and memories, ID, Lower third in the past

Each zone represents a particular aspect of an individual. The ratio between them indicates the writer's preferences.

Normal balance If all zones are the same proportions, it indicates that the writer is a balanced person. He is attentive to every element of his existence.

An overexaggeration in one region can result in a reduction in the other. A zone can also become disorganized or be entangled in the adjacent zone. This could indicate that the individual is experiencing problems with a specific portion of themselves. Certain illnesses can be the cause and the abnormal area often indicates the area of the body where it's.

The upper portion is composed from the letter bizonal b D, H, K and the letter l. Particularly, the top portions that contain the letters H, and T belong to the upper zones.

The middle zone contains all vowels (a, e, i and u, o,) and consonants such as c, m, n and

s. They also have r, V, W and x. They are only written inside the middle zone.

The lower part of the zone contains the bizonal letters: g, J, p, Q as well as y and z.

The sole trizonal letter of the alphabet is the letter f.

Upper Zone

The height of the upper zone reflects how much a person requires to be stimulated intellectually.

Upper zone length: demonstrates how intensely a person feels the urge.

The high upper strokes are a re-enactment of an individual's efforts to move toward an objective. If these strokes are extended the person could be making unrealistic goals.

If the upper zone loops are proportional in relation to other text, the writer is likely to be able to balance the need for ambition with a sense of humour.

Large upper zone loops are indications they are enthralled by their dreams and is thinking about them frequently. If they are unusually large, it could indicate that the person attempts to present an appearance of intellectual proficiency to cover up feelings of inferiority. They could be susceptible to exaggerations too.

If the upward stroke is angled upwards and then back down the person may be suffocating their daydreams in order to focus on their responsibilities in the real world.

Strokes that sway upwards are an indication of the writer's efforts to show off his/her intellect. They are frequently observed in performers.

Upper zone that is tangled: If the upper zone gets tangled with the line in front of that, then the author might be distracted by some problem within his or her life. There could be lots going on in their heads and this can cause creative thinking.

Exaggerated upper zones A writer may be smart and ambitious, however, he or she may not be able to translate concepts into reality. If the exaggeration is too extreme (too detailed, high or deformed) it could mean that the writer may live in a fantasy world.

Lower upper zone The person might prefer practical things over dreams and theories. If other characteristics of the writing suggest an excellent character, a smaller upper area could mean that the person is realistic. If there are indicators that indicate the deceitfulness of the person it could indicate that the person is not a moral person.

Middle Zone

Wide middle area: Determines the degree of confidence a person feels in asking what they wants

The middle zone represents the person's self-image. It provides information on what the writer's behavior is in public. This is important to their standing in the workplace, school at a company, in business or church, as well as in other situations where he or she is exposed to others.

The size of the letters in the middle area will reveal how the writer handles his or her moods. If the middle zone has different-sized letters, then the individual may be struggling to control emotions.

In the middle zone, breaks in letters can be caused by interruptions during writing. This could be due to stress and anxiety.

A knotted middle zone indicates ineffectiveness and lack of discipline. If there are numerous loops, the writer could be able to enjoy a good relationship with others but could be dishonest when managing the loops.

An exaggerated middle zone writer is self-centered and focuses too much on his or her self. They can even be impulsive.If the writing style is not impressive and focuses on the middle area this indicates perfectionist. The writer adheres to the rules which means that the writing does not deviate away from the center.

Lower Zone

The width of the lower zone exposes the level of creativity as well as productivity

The lower part of the brain is the domain of the subconscious as well as the instinctual drive.

A straight downward stroke means impatience.

A full lower loop written in a forceful manner indicates that the author is a person with a positive attitude. The energy could mean many things: the writer could be business-minded, athletic, sensual, and much more. Other elements in the text will indicate the purpose for which energy is being used to serve.

The complete loop written in a light manner reveals an interest in more security.

An upper loop which is huge and resembles a purse is a symbol of greed for the writer.

Retraced lower zones: When strokes in the lower zone are drawn not using loops or downward lines, but instead with curves, the author may be stopping past trauma from coming into the consciousness of. It can be difficult to establish a relationship with the writer since they are attempting to protect themselves from becoming at risk.

A lower stroke which resembles the shape of a cradle indicates a need to stay clear of fights.

If you notice different forms in the lower region The writer could be in emotional turmoil. Other characteristics of the writing will provide additional details regarding this.

Exaggeration of the lower zone: A writer is driven by basic desires. The large loops of this zone represent a sense of agitation and a desire to satisfy your cravings. It could also indicate the person has a high level of energy, but the person might lack the self-control and vision to manage this energy effectively.

A decreased lower zone A writer might be scared of something. They may also feel unbalanced. Sexual issues and the past might be present.

The proportions of Erratic zones

Inconsistent ratios reveal the confusion of priorities as well as the instability of character.

Summary

The middle, upper, and lower writing zones reflect the writer's feelings, thoughts physical and emotional urges. A larger area in one indicates a focal point in that specific area.

Margins

Margins are associated with certain concerns that writers face and the kind of margin used by a writer reveals the attitudes he/she has towards these issues.

Left margins

The left side is associated to the previous. This is the case for the person's birthplace as well as relationship with his parents.

It's easier to make an even left margin contrast to creating straight right margins. Due to this, the left margin is a symbol of an ideal self, while the right is the real self.

If the left margin is large, the writer is looking to move away from the events that have occurred before and continue on.

If it's restricted, the writer is not happy being pressured.

A rigid left margin is a sign that it's difficult to keep an aesthetically aligned margin an unruly left margin indicates an urgent desire to maintain order. The person is full of self-control and is aware of the consequences of every decision. They are also very self-conscious and stern with other people because they are aware of the ideals and expectations.

Incorrect left margin: When the left margin appears to be haphazard it means that the person isn't aware of expectations and rules. Also, he/she lacks willpower and can be easily affected. They make decisions at will, with no thought of the consequences.

Shrinking left margin

If the left margin is initially large, but slowly moves closer to the left side that is the edge of paper. The author might be filled with enthusiasm and confidence at first but this decreases as time goes by. This can be an indication of fatigue, due to the need to expend excessive energy in a short period of time. They may also want to go back in time or an old circumstance.

Margin for growth of left

If the left margin becomes larger as it advances The writer starts with caution, but the determination grows the more engaged in something. This could mean that the writer could be in excess of resources.

Margin left of concave (curves to the left, pointing towards the middle)

This is evident in writers who have fought the temptation to overspend, but is able to control it at the end.

Left margin convex (bows outwards from the middle)

Writers who have these kinds of profits are those who are aware they have to be in control of how much they spend However, they tend to lose track of time and.

There is no margin (the writing occupied the entire page) The term "no margins" can refer to a variety of things, including thriftiness and an acceptance of past as well as the future, or an absence of the boundaries. What it means can be identified by different forms of penmanship.

Right Margin

This is connected to the future. It is also a sign of how a person interacts with others.

If the margin of right is within the margin the person is excited about the future and prepared for whatever comes next.

If the margin of safety is a long way from an edge could suggest that the person isn't prepared to face the challenges of tomorrow and prefers to remain with what he/she currently is aware of.

Top Margin

The margin on the top describes the individual's hopes, desires and hopes, as well as dreams and goals. It also indicates how much the individual respects the person he/she writes to.

Large higher margin: A wide top margin can be a sign of respect to the person the writer has written his or her letter. It could also indicate that the person has a respectable character generally.

The narrow upper margin A narrow or insignificant top margin could indicate disrespect. Otherwise, he/she may be disinterested in formalities and prefers being straight-to-the-point.

Bottom Margin

The bottom margin reveals the writer's realism, intuitions and enthusiasm.

A broad bottom margin could indicate that the writer is no longer interested in the practical aspects. They have a detached outlook and is focused more on ideals and not paying attention to what's happening around them. The person may be deficient in confidence and avoidance from people.

A small bottom margin may symbolize pragmatism and materialism. The person may also wish to be more expressive, such as in the manner they tried to fit words on the space. If other signs are indicating sadness, it may be an indication of depressive symptoms (sadness is a feeling of heavyness and the hand could be pulled downwards). The person may also be sceptical of something and so remains near towards the floor (the lowest point section of the webpage).

There are no Margins

A writer who cannot stay in one location. The writer has a mind that is constantly active which is not confined by conventions.

Large margins all around

The writer sees the paper as a canvas which is a frame for pictures. The writer may have an artistic brain which is extremely particular about design and style. The artist may also be cautious when it comes to finances. The writing on the left illustrates the need to pool resources into an area that is safe.

Summary

The margins symbolize what's happened in the present (left margin) as well as in the near future (right margin) respect (top margin) along with vitality (bottom margin). The way that the text interacts with the margins reveals the writer's attitudes towards these topics.

Spacing

Word spacings, line spacings and letter spacings speak of the writer's ability to manage time space, resources, and space. They also show how the writer interacts with different situations and people.

Line spacing

Line spacing requires the ability to be able to effectively manage time and accurately estimate space. It also indicates whether the person is clear in their thinking or not.

It is ideal if the paper you are looking at is not lined because lined paper creates an order to the writing, and stops the natural writing form being visible.

Clear line spacing

This is a sign of mental clarity and the ability to organize. The writer is organized and is able to make use of resources efficiently. The writer is also a smart decision maker.

Wide line spacing

Lines that are separated from one another are typically created by people who prefer to be secluded and take a wider view. They plan ahead and allow plenty of time to deal with unpredictable situations. They don't act in a hurry, but thinks about the possible outcomes of their actions before taking anything. This could be an indication that the author is rich and doesn't have any issues spending greater than the typical person.

Very wide line spacing

The writer who is known for using excessive amount of spacing between his lines does not like crowds. They are always anxious. The reason is that he/she isn't able to see the whole pictureand is overwhelmed by the tiny things that don't make sense.

Narrow line spacing

Lines that are closely spaced are created with a writer that dives to the story and is involved in the events. If this is the case alongside loosely structured writing, it suggests a person who is able to handle stressful situations. It could also indicate that the person is conscious of the necessity of conserving resources and time. The person may not want to spending money unless there is an urgent need to.

Extremely thin line spacing

The writer who makes lines get in the way of each other is an impulsive individual who is not able to think rationally. They are extremely impulsive and is prone to saying or doing things completely out of the blue. The person may also speak or act faster than they might think due to inability to see ahead.

Tangled lines

When loops intersect with parts of the letters that appear on the next lines, the person writing may have a hard time keeping the situation in check. They are having trouble keeping control and is prone to be more involved than what is feasible for him/her. Conflicts with self as well as with other people are also a frequent event.

Irregular line spacing

This reveals the writer's inconsistent methods of dealing with time, wealth, and space. If the spacing displays an evolution in the same way, it is also indicative of the gradual shift in the person's attitude. For instance, if the spacing is clear at first, but is narrower, the person might begin the process in a calm way and then become more agitated as he/she gets further into a particular project or circumstance.

Line spacing is extremely regular.

Regular line spacing is the best But too much of it causes issues. It reveals rigidity and perfectionists. It will be difficult to get the writer to change his/her the routine and standards of his/her own.

Word Spacing

Word spacing represents the need to maintain social distance. Allotting spaces between written words is similar to pausing between spoken sentences. The longer the pause, the more at ease the writer feels communicating with others.

Find out the width average of each letter, and then compare this with the space between words.

Word spacing that is balanced

The writer is at ease with himself/herself and is respectful of the rights of others and rights. The writer abides by the rules of the organization he/she belongs within.

Wide word spacing

It is a writer who thinks before committing to an idea. The writer is less reserved and the more spontaneous. The circle of friends he/she has may be small , but tight-knit.

Word spacing is extremely wide.

Words that are far from each other tell others to remain in their own space. It also indicates issues with the writer's ability to organize thoughts into an order and to express them clearly. Writers may experience intense anxiety-related feelings that keep them from socializing or thinking clearly.

Word spacing that is narrow

The narrow spaces indicate someone who enjoys being in a group. If the person's handwriting is simple and uncareful, they could be a bit snarky and do don't respect the boundaries of other people.

The extremely narrow spacing of words is an absolute disregard for limits. The writer is driven by the desire to be in a group with other people. However, they lack a perception of the inner world also - in their mind there is nothing in the person to investigate. Therefore, this writer might be unable to see the bigger picture and appear as being shallow. They may also be completely dependent on others.

Uneven word spacing

This indicates a skewed approach to social interaction. The person may also be experiencing internal conflicts. If the other indicators in the handwriting prove it, this word spacing could indicate restlessness and a lack of self-control.

Letter Spacing

The spaces between letters indicate the degree of acceptance by the writer of his/her self. This is the individual's internal space that allows him/her to become more open to both external and personal stimuli. The number of spaces indicates how much space the writer makes for himself or herself.

Wide letter spacing

The wide spacing of letters is typical when writing with wide letters. If both spaces and letters are large, the author is lively and spontaneous. They are sociable and easy to be around.

Space between letters is narrow

If letters are joined it is possible that the person could feel internal pressure. This is why he/she could be more likely to react too quickly and assess situations or people early. The person is pressured to conform within an environment to the point that he/she does things that make him uncomfortable. The person may suddenly explode at any time.

Irregular letter spacing

Letters that are close to each the other at certain points, but distant at other times indicate issues in the writer's internal space. The writer may not know how to proceed, at the very least, in the moment writing the draft.

Spaces that are wide and narrow letters between them

The person who writes pretends to be outgoing , but within, he/she really is an introvert. The writer may be attempting to be social with others.

Summary

Spacings show how the writer separates himself/herself from people and the environment. The bigger the space more necessity for solitude.

Pressure

The force wrote with is considered to be interpreted. The force can be measured by watching the person write and noting how deep the writing marks appear on paper.

Heavy pressure

The forceful strokes of the body show that the person is serious about commitments. He is a spirited and long-lasting.

The extremely heavy strokes show the strict and temperamental nature.

Light strokes indicate the sensitivity and permeability.

The absence of pressure in the extremities is an indication that the individual is weak.

The pressure on the writing surface is monitored by:

* The intensity and darkness of the ink
* The thickness of the writing or the depth at which the pen penetrated the paper (this is visible across the surface of paper)

It is important to understand what type of writing instrument employed to avoid conflating the kind of ink used with the type of pressure employed.

Thickness

The sharpness or fuzziness the strokes reveals the sexuality of the individual.

"fine" means sensitivity; lack of desire for sensuality spiritually-oriented

* Medium: sensuality that is balanced and temperance
* Heavy materialism, sensuality, love of the senses and dominance

Summary

Pressure represents writers' potential power. A high level of pressure can be an indication of tension whereas the lightness of pressure is a sign sadness or weakness. A moderately high level of pressure is linked to healthy health.

Connectedness

Connecting shapes are symbolic of ways that the author connects his thoughts and manages effort, handles emotions and operates in relational relationships.

Connected

You could say that handwriting is connected if the words of eight letters or less are joined. If breaks occur there are breaks only after syllables or after I dots and t cross. When letters are separated then the writing becomes disconnected.

Connected: employs logic in making decisions and conclusions is consistent, puts the best interests of self over others

Disconnected letters favor the intuition and feelings over logic, takes into account the opinions and ideas of others

Connective forms

These are the links between one letter and the next. It is easy to spot these on the tops of lowercase letters m and N.

Arcade

If the majority of connective shapes include arches (rounded tops) The writer is emotionally tense, but hides the emotion. Arcades that are written in a fast pace involve upward motion, which demonstrates the writer's drive to do things. Arcades that are slow can be associated with dishonesty because the shrewdness, ambition and concealment can be deceitful.

Garland

Connective forms which are generally garlands indicate that the writer is pleasant and friendly. If garlands are designed using a weak pressure or drooping strokes, the writer could be depressed or passive. If the garlands loop to on the left side, then the person may be feeling stressed and they seek to release tension by moving into the inside.

An Angular

Angles are formed by abrupt stops and shifts in direction. They are produced using rigid motions. This means that the writer will be a rigid person and also inflexible. They make the choices rather than submitting to others' wishes. Pressured angles that are too high can be a sign of the ugliness of. When angles appear rounded the writer's whims are tempered by kindness. Bending angles show a dual-sided personality - the author appears friendly, yet can become angry when challenged.

Thread

Threads are a fusion version of garland and arcade. Since it's difficult to write threads at a slow pace, it typically suggests a quick thinker.

Thready writing can be a sign of intelligence. If the writing is thin, it may be a sign of anxiety and lack of resoluteness.

Mixed

Garland/angle: A writer's formidable willpower is balanced by compassion.

Garland/arcade: The author is open-minded and critical and balances informality with spontaneity.

Angle/thread The angle/thread combination since it mixes deceit and abrasiveness.

Combination of all

This is an indication of a person who's flexible and able to adapt to various situations.

The strokes that begin and end are also instructive.

Beginning strokes

* Few: efficient

* Hooks * Hooks

* Simple: efficient

* Looped: conceit

Ending strokes

* Falling: depressed

* Heavy The word "heavy" means brutal.

* Short for: thrifty

* Wavy: funny

Summary

The degree of connection and the kind of connective forms reveal how the writer interacts with others. Beginning and ending strokes reveal information about the persona of the writer.

Slant

The angle or the degree to which the letters tilt relative to the baseline can tell you about the person's emotions. In general the more the letters lean toward the right side of the paper the more emotional person is.

Letters that have upper loops like b, d and k. and t are able to tell you the grade and orientation of the writing.

Upright letters: independence and objectiveness. Flexible to the current situation but cautious with the actions and decisions. The writer prefers to think over feelings.

Inclinated (leaning toward the right) A desire to take action on objectives and to respond to the world around you. The tendency to experience immediate responses to events.

* Slightly leaning to the right Want to connect with other people
* Leaning slightly towards the right: sympathy emotionality
* Extremely leaning towards the right: recklessness and fanaticism.

Reclined (leaning towards the left) The writer is stuck into the past. Is unable to react to events in a timely manner.

* Slightly leaning towards the left: caution and self-centeredness.

* Leaning slightly towards the left, self-consciousness inner turmoil

* Extremely leaning to the left Repression, withdrawal or seclusion

Varying (combination of reclined, upright and inclined) In the event that there is no consistent pattern of slanting, it indicates an unpredictability and instability for the artist.

Handwritings can have varying angles, but they are consistent with the general trend:

The person starts upright, but leans towards the right over time The individual begins as a reserved individual, but then becomes more social later on.

The writer starts upright, but he leans to the extreme right at some point The writer tries to maintain control, but soon loses control.

Starts to tilt to the right, but then becomes more upright The person may initially be exuberant, but then becomes more calm.

A sudden change in the direction of a word could indicate that the writer is not comfortable in the particular word. It could also mean it is a sign that the author may be not telling the truth.

One upright term in an generally inclined script. writer is hesitant concerning the word.

A single reclined word within an otherwise upright script The word can trigger intense emotions for the writer.

Lower zones that reach towards the left: If letters' tails of the letters tilt towards the right rather than toward the left it indicates that sexual urges and instincts are suppressed.

Lower zones that reach to the left In the event that the tails of the letters are extending towards the left side, then the author relies on others to satisfy their requirements. They may seek an ideal mother persona.

Variable: Slants that vary reflect an exuberant and unstable temperament.

Summary

Slants indicate an expressiveness and sociability. Slanting to the right indicates being more social and outgoing and moving to the left signifies the opposite. A slant that is upright means that there is an equilibrium between these two extremes. Slants in other sections of the text may also indicate something, so take them into consideration too.

Baseline

The baseline slant refers to the direction in which the letters are positioned in relation with the base (written or imagined) beneath them. This is a way to show the writer's goal-orientedness and how they approach goals. The base represents a symbolic representation of objectives and goals, and the written letters speak for the person's actions as well as behavior.

Slant upwards

When sentences and words are positioned in such that they appear to be lifted off of the base line, this indicates writers are typically optimistic. They may also rely on their intuition when making decisions and acting.

Slant downward

If the lines of writing are slanted downwards, so that the words at the end have a lower level than their baseline line of writing, the author could be tired or pessimistic. The writer may also be directing the way he/she reacts.

Even baseline

If the writer is written before, it might indicate that they are a successful goal-seeker. They are likely to have the ability to control emotions and keep a steady focus to meet goals.

Uneven baseline

If lines move upwards and downwards like waves that writer may be prone to a sense of restlessness. They may be unable to stay in the right direction and controlling their moods.

Lines arched

The writer is extremely energetic initially, but the energy decreases gradually.

Concave lines

The writer could lose focus and energy during the course of work but he/she is determined to finish what they have started. It could also be a sign of courage.

Steps that fall

If the words or portions of sentences are tilting downwards, the patient is probably trying to get over depression or lethargy.

Steps to the right

When the words or portions of sentences are inclined upwards The writer is trying to control his/her excitement and confidence.
The increase of certain sentence or sentence part or word

This could be a deliberate or subconscious attempt to emphasize the text. Maybe the author is pleased with it and wants the reader to pay attention to the text. Perhaps, the writer is enjoying the experience.
An egress of specific sentence/sentence component/word

It is also a result of paying more emphasis on the text, but the emotions that are behind it tend to be negative. If not, the author might not be comfortable speaking about the sentiment.
Summary
The baseline is tied to goals and the location of the text relative to it indicates an the attitude toward the goals. When a word is elevated or is dropped from the baseline, the focus is paid to it.
Size
The letters' sizes are representations of the self-image.

In average, handwritten letters measure 9 millimeters. Normal-sized letters are written by a calm and considerate person. They could also be traditional.

Small writing may be a sign of someone who thinks and is more than emotion.

Small and thin lines indicate a timid nature.

A large font is a sign of a confident and outgoing persona.

Penmanship that is excessively large can result from an image of self-esteem that is too big.

The letters can be of different sizes written by a person with an unorthodox persona.

Summary

Utilize the measuring ruler that measures 9 millimeters. Then examine it against how large the writing. It is possible to determine how much the writer views his or her writing by the size of his or her handwriting is.

Specific Letters

Particular letters can tell you the character of a writer.

Loops L (lowercase)

* Narrow: tense person

* Wide: person who is relaxed who can express himself or herself freely

E (lowercase)

The small e symbolises listening capability. Look at the loop of the e. A wide e is suitable for someone who listens effectively. A tight E is for someone who does not listen.

I (lowercase)

* Normally bigger that the other writing arrogance

* Normal or smaller: Average the ego

* Looped I: ambitious, relaxed, spontaneous

The dots (lowercase)

The normal place (right over the I stem) A well-organized and paying particular attention to details

* High above I stem a vast imagination

* Slashed in the sense of being critical about oneself and others and impatient

* Circled I: visionary, childlike, artistic and seeks attention

* Dots: neat, attention to detail

* Left of I The left of i is procrastination, or nervousness

* Jabbed to gossip

* Tent like: humorous

* I dots are missing the word carelessness

T (lowercase)

The T stem

The height of the t stem is the writer's pride in their work.

A moderately high stem If the t stem is more than twice the height of the middle zone the person is at ease with oneself and is assertive when required.

Extremely tall t-stem The t stem is 2.5 times higher than the middle zone suggests a self-centered and proud nature. The author might also have a father who is demandingand wants to please him. Therefore, they boast about their achievements.

Short T stem: The author is satisfied with their work and doesn't seek approval from others.

Normal stem of t The t stem that conforms to the copybook style can be executed by someone who is a follower of the rules, and by other people.

Looped t stemsof t: A large loop can be an indication of the sensitivity. If the T stems are looped the writer might be too sensitive about their work. The writer isn't able to deal with criticism and might be fearful.

Cross T (lower case)

The size of the t's cross-section on the stem shows the level at which the writer's objectives are. In graphology crossing the t, it aligns the person with reality since it's in line with the baseline which is the reality.

Height of the copybook: The person is able to set goals for himself or herself that they is able to achieve.

Very low T-cross that is extremely low could be a sign of depression or a the inability to reach goals. The person writing it may lack confidence and desire. It could also indicate that the writer just completed a task and needs to rest for a time.

High T: A t over the normal line indicates a person with goals that are high. The writer continuously improves his or her capabilities and is determined to reach his/her goals.

The topmost point of the stem, or over that: If high t crosses are very few, this indicates that the writer has a tendency to think ahead. If there are too many of them, it means that the writer isn't being realistic.

T cross length (lowercase)

A look at the length of the t-bar indicates the amount of energy and determination the writer puts in achieving their objectives.

Average cross length of t This demonstrates the practicality and reliability. Since it is a Copybook design, this indicates the standardization.

Short-t cross: The writer may be lazy and unmotivated. The writer is weak and insecure.

Long T cross: This shows an author with a strong will who isn't afraid to make use of force to obtain what she wants. They can also be a leader for others.

Extremely long cross-section It is a sign to watch out for the tendency to bully.

A long and pointed t cross is executed with rage While a lengthy and heavy t-cross exposes the brutality.

T Cross Pressure

The pressure of the t cross shows the level of energy of the person who is achieving goals.

Strong T Cross: A solid t cross indicates that the author has the ability to conquer obstacles that hinder his or her objectives.

Weak cross The reason for this is the writer who quickly gets exhausted and gives up too soon.

Cross-over from strong to weak The writing process begins with intense pressure but slows down in a gradual manner, the writer may also start with intense conviction, but it will diminish over time.

Strong to weak t cross: This could indicate that the writer develops more confidence and motivation as they get closer to achieving the goal.

T cross slant (lowercase)

T crosses tilt downwards A normal t-cross that is slanting down could mean assertiveness. However, when it is written with a lot of pressure, it could suggest dominance rather than.

T crosses with a slant they signify optimism as well as enthusiasm and ambition.

Other T crosses

Concave T cross (bowing downwards) T crosses that appear like they're pressed to the center indicate that the writer is an over-commitment.

Convex T crosses (bowing upwards) T crosses that curvature up as arches are a sign that the author is protecting themselves from being swindled by. The writer will usually refuse any assistance from others and will do things in the way that suits them.

T-cross on the left side of the stem. Cautiousness is known to slow down the writer's hand and lead to the creation of these t cross.

T crosses to the right end of the stem. Excitedness within a writer triggers the writer to create this type of T's.

T crosses in the middle When the t cross is in the exact center of the stem the writer is extremely precise and precise.

A t-stem that is not crossed It could mean the absence of care or procrastination.

Sharply pointed t bars T bars that appear sharp are a sign of sarcasm or verbal attacks from the writing profession.

T bars attached to the stem, or the following letter. The person who designs these t's are clever and creative.

Lasso loops t's: If the t bars are reminiscent of Lassos due to the fact that they go to the left and loops on the right side, the author may be feeling guilt over something. They may find themselves constantly going back on the past their mind.

T's are crossed two times: An individual with obsessive-compulsive disorder may write t's in this the way.

T cross Wavy: Wavy T bars could be made by an eccentric person.

X

The x may reveal a variety of things regarding the author. If the x does not have a cross indicates negligence. If it's bent the writer yields easily to pressure, whereas an uncrossed x could be a sign of insolence.

The Xs on a checkbox will let you know if an individual is focused on the past or the future If it's on the left, the person is anchored to the past. While on the right, he/she is excited about the future.

K (lowercase)

It is possible to think of the lowercase letter k as a character as well as a pair of wide arms.

A k that has a cross bar that is looped around the stem can be done by someone who is affectionate. It's similar to hugging someone with arms.

A K that has crossed bars located far off from its stem can be done by someone who is not comfortable with physical contact with other people.

A k that has crossed bars that cut through the stem signifies aggression which could be self-directed as it's directed to one side (which is the direction of self).

A capital letter placed in a location that is intended to lowercase indicates it's a sign that the person writing the letter is rebellious. The writer isn't shy about bringing attention to themselves.

Wiggly k. When the k does not have any cross bars however it has lines that are wavy and the writer is unsteady and manipulative.

The letters M as well as N (lowercase)

The way the letters are styled indicates thinking styles.

Round tops are created by people who accumulate knowledge and accumulate past experiences and knowledge, and then connect them to the latest information.

The sharply-pointed tops of the ear are often associated with thinkers who are investigative. They seek out the reasons and the meaning behind things. The upward movement is a subconscious desire to take a look at the bigger view.

Pointed bottoms with sharp edges are connected to the analytical mind. They are a symbol of digging actions to discover facts or to examine the details.

Top that is thready

This is a mindset that is often superficial since it only scratches the surface of the world.

M (lowercase)

* Looks like a letter u: friendly
* First M stroke high arrogant

Letter P

The letter P is a lower-zone letter, which is why it is usually connected to physicality.

Long loop A writer is a lover of physical activity. The writer may play sports.

A rounded top was composed by those who are devoted to harmony.

The stroke is tall: If a person has a straight and tall stroke that is extending into the upper region and is a lover of debates and arguments.

Large lower loop The lower loop appears like balloons, then the person might be deceitful, or even promise to keep promises they don't honor. They might also be sexually flirtatious , but do not follow through with their actions.

R (lowercase)

It looks like reverse 3: Making this kind of shape requires attention. The person who is writing the letter r is one who is conscious of their appearance and will put in the effort to appear attractive.

Flat Top: It is intended for builders who are proficient using tools and performing manual work.

Sharp Top: This upward motion suggests an intelligent person who is keen on learning new things.

Round top: The top that is round suggests a person is content with what he/she already knows and doesn't generally look further into the matter.

Printing: If the letter written cursive, then the person writing it is imaginative and can think of things in a different way.

G (lowercase)

A g formed like the number eight indicates a person who's skilled at writing and is funny. The writer is a fast thinker , who might also enjoy philosophy too.

D (lowercase)

Extra high stem Arrogance

Lowercase letters a, o and e

In the middle, there is a zone connected to communication, and the letters such as a, o, and e indicate how someone communicates and listens to other people.

The lowercase letters a's, letters with o's and e's represent the individual's willingness to speak with others. Examine on the outside of the letters in order to see how open the person is. If you see strange lines or the writer is having difficulties with their expression. It could be that the writer is lying or has difficulties putting thoughts into words.

The open: They are able to easily communicate with others and be expressive of their feelings. On the other hand they're not very good in keeping secrets.

Open tops with wide open sides: They are usually done by gossipers and loud mouths.

Closed: The individual is secretive and restricts self-expression.

Lower case letter 'a' and an overspray above: The person might be dealing with issues they don't want to discuss. It could also be an indication of artistic talent Check for other creative ways or indications of distress to figure out what is which.

A or o which forms an entire circle: The writer is inclined to stay away from the topic. The writer may go for hours without ever getting to the core.

Extra loops

A loop left-hand side of an o could mean that the person is denial of something to himself or herself. When it's located on the opposite side it means that the person might be hiding some thing from others. The loops that are on the opposite side reveal the ugliness of a person.

If the loops are within the letter o or a the writer is experiencing pent-up emotions. The writer will not want to discuss them.

They could also indicate obstructions in communication. The writer might be having trouble communicating however feels that something is preventing him or her from communicating.

Hooks: Hooks in A's and O's are indicators of bad communication habits. This could mean that the writer is inclined to verbally attack other people or to lie frequently.

B (lowercase)

The lowercase letter b reveals the trustworthiness of a person.

*Open b: A writer is a believer easily.

* Closed b If the b is small, the person could be skeptical.

S (lowercase)

"Round": is a way make people happy and prevents conflict.

* Pointy: intellectual the level of sharpness of your eyes reveals the ambition level as well as inquisitiveness

" Wide in the lower right could be sacrificed to what the writer really wants.

Y

* Big looped Y: confident. have many friends

* LongY: adventurous, loves travelling

Capitals

* Tall: assertive

The tallest and most exaggerated arrogance

Summary

Take note of these letters I, e, the letters t, x as well as m, n P, r, g as well as d O, b, the letters s and y How they are written will provide clues to the person who wrote them.

Capital letters also show how much pride an individual takes in their work.

Signatures

The subconscious association of a person's signature with their identity. So, signatures reveal many aspects of personality and self-perception. The way the writer views his family as well as his/her spouse can also be revealed.

Private person who isn't readable does not like being read

Legitimate: authentic and confident

Large letters The person who thinks highly of themselves

Small: defensive, lacks self-confidence

It's not sound like formal or first names.

Unreadable or no last name: might be having issues with family

More extensive than the rest of text and more Exciting

Signatures with a unique design: to be acknowledged

Signed in a circle A desire to be secured

A line that crosses the signature is a way of cancelling one's identity. If it is crossed by the name or is the signature of a woman who is married, she might have issues with her husband.

A stroke that is not covered by the signature. The person writing it is trying to protect his or her self from something. If the line is placed under your signature could indicate that the writer is trying to hide something from the past.

Signatures that have a dot at the end of the signature: A signal that the person signing the signature is wary or has had an problem that he or she cannot let go of.

Signature is smaller than the all the script The writer is not estimating the extent of his or her anger or is trying to appear less modest than who he or she really is.

A very rising signature could be trying to avoid an eventuality that events may not go as planned they'd like

Underlined: Conceit

Summary

The signature is a representation of the individual who wrote it. It is a reflection of how the person perceives the persona of their identity as well as how he/she is related to family or to the spouse.

Warning Signs on Writing

The writing of a person can reveal the negative aspects of a person.

Immaturity

In writing, it is evident that the writer is not mature with t-crosses that are poorly drawn and loops that are swollen.

Self-critical

Self-criticism is portrayed as unnecessary dots in the base, hooked and the slashing strokes.

Deceit

These are indicators of deceit by a writer:

* If letters are crowded together or not aligned along with other sentences.

* Small e's curled

"Cover strokes": When the loop appears to be one line, the writer performed an abrupt motion with their hand. It is similar to rapid changes in thought , which can be a sign of dishonesty.

* Cover strokes on middle zone letters signal the denial of the truth.

* Arcades placed on top of characters or towards the bottom of a words (curling in the direction of the right) is a method of trying to cover up or hide the truth.

The Wavy Baseline: demonstrates an absence of reliability, and could also indicate lying

• Counterstrokes when the strokes are made from the reverse direction to the direction they are supposed to be

* Patched and smashed up strokes: A sign that the author is trying to make up for inconsistent writing by presenting an untrue image

* Coiled forms signify vanity and the necessity to shield oneself from the burdens of life

* Forms that are too complicated Although complicated forms can be a sign of creativity, they could also indicate a need conceal details or divert viewers from seeing what they ought to be looking at.

Double loops Double loops indicate the extra effort used to embellish or conceal something.

* Letters missing: If writing is slow the writer has left important details

• Ending strokes that are terminated suspended, not returning to the baseline deliberately omitting details

* Letters that look like others: try to alter and misrepresent an event

Signature form is not comparable to the rest of text: The author is not genuine

* If you notice random lines in oval letters the author could be an regular lying.

Grudges

Double loops that appear to be hooks could be a sign of taking or retaining the past issues.

Verify that the left margin of the page is narrow and if it is, then the author hasn't moved on yet.

Dr. Jekyll-Mr. Hyde Syndrome

If the lowercase d or an upper-zone letter suddenly falls over to the left the letter, it indicates an explosive behaviour for someone who is otherwise a good person. After the incident the behavior, the person is able to return to a calm, relaxed manner and acts as if nothing has was happening.

Double Crosser

Be on the lookout for these letters: m.n the letters r as well as s and w. The last strokes of these could bend in a different way or bow towards the opposite of the direction it is expected to go. These are indications that the person writing is a double-crosser.

Evasiveness

The e that begins with a straight line that is hidden by a curve represents an action that suddenly stopped and then redirected to the opposite direction. This reveals a personality who is deliberate and devious.

If the g is a narrow loop as well as an upstroke that looks like an inverse C, the author could be deceitful and concealing his/her self-centered motives.

Handwriting that is not legible: If penmanship is difficult to read it could be a sign it is because the author has been trying the best they can to not be "read".

Violence

These alerts will warn you about aggressive tendencies.

* Extremely high pressure: The writer is afflicted with intense feelings which can be released through insensitive or violent acts

Variable pressure: Unpredictability and inconsistency could be a sign of an unsteady mind.

* Extreme Right Slant The disregard for the boundaries of one's life and an abundance emotion and energy

* Dots that are heavy: signify guilt, tension, or a covering up of information

*Slashing strokes downwards strokes that are heavy and then taper off indicate an angry and verbally abusive personality

"Club Strikes," a sudden increase in thickness at the end of strokes. It could refer to verbal assaults for those in the middle zone , or physical attacks if located in lower areas.

* T-crosses that are strange They are a sign that the author is not having problem doing anything to assist the writer get what he

desires even if it is morally wrong or illegal actions.

* Hooks that are positioned under the base: They are symbols of violent impulses hidden in the background that are then acted out

* Extremely angular forms such as aggressive tendencies

* Narrow forms such as antisocial personality

Unpredictability

Abnormal rhythm: lack of harmony both in attitude and behavior

A recurring rising in letters The person is usually quiet, but is suddenly aggressive at times.

Capitals with curly letters in middle words: author uses inappropriate actions to attract the attention of others.

Inconsistent styles: Unpredictability

Summary

The study of graphology can tell if the writer is exhibiting undesirable characteristics. Look for the characteristics listed above and compare them with other traits of penmanship.

Infections

A person's health is evident in the penmanship of a person that is consistent in pressure, free and relaxed strokes, well-placed spacing and writing zones that are equally proportioned.

The effects of specific injuries alter the penmanship within the writing zones , which correspond to the body part or parts.

Headache, toothache or sore throat, as well as other conditions that affect the upper region of the body could be represented by a dot or s in the upper region.

The mid-section of your body could be identified by irregularities in the middle zone letters of various dimensions and/or shapes broken forms, fractures that are being retraced or threaded (fading to thin lines) or in lower-than-normal postures.

Generalized ailments are seen in the general penmanship

The blood pressure of high pressure The writing indicates different pressures are being used The written material appears dark in certain areas and bright in other

* Heart disease or circulatory conditions: random ink blots onto the papers, slow speeds unstable pressure, tangling letters bent strokes

* Nerve injury: varying pressures, irregular strokes, lines with a narrow spacings, wrote at a slow pace and rigid letters

* Schizophrenia: various angles indicate a disconnect from reality
* Alzheimer's disease: shaking writing, strange letters
* Parkinson's Disease: very tiny writing
* Down syndrome writing disintegrated
* Mental impairment Writing skeletally

Alcohol and drugs can cause handwriting to become muddled. Penmanship can have minor deviations in line spacing, letter size and forms, as well as baselines. Connecting strokes might not easily flow into letters. More powerful substances trigger trembling handwriting as well as sudden shifts in pressure, slant, and letter form. The handwriting will be irregular and full of mistakes.

Psychological reactions to the illness

The t bars of sick patients may grow longer than normal as they try to beat the disease.

Fear of dying or illness could cause writers to ignore particular details like i-dots or T-crosses.

Being aware of your body may result in the appearance of larger lower loops.

The physical and psychological pain can manifest in penmanship, unsteady writing or different pressures onto the papers.

The signs of depression in penmanship can also be a sign of illness.

Important: To determine if you have a medical condition or abuse of substances to determine the cause of a problem, you must have several writing samples from various periods of time. This can help you figure out if the writing characteristics are natural or triggered by a underlying condition.

Summary

Penmanship characteristics can reveal a variety of ailments however, make sure you look over various writing samples of the same person to exclude the possibility of temporary influences.

Specific Traits

Certain personality traits will appear as a feature or combination of characteristics in penmanship.

Aggressiveness: straight and diagonal upstrokes

Caring: a combination of thread and garland

Commitment: neat middle zone

Confidence: loose script, medium pressure

Decisiveness: straight downstrokes

The best: a good management of space, not overcrowded or separated too much

Gentleness: Light to medium pressure

Excellent communication abilities: developed lower zone with large strokes

Self-esteem and health: normal rhythm

Honesty A moderate and even rhythm

Humor: legible signature

Intelligence: simplified letter forms

Intimacy: medium to narrow word spacing and thick strokes

In love with flowing forms

People-orientation: Medium to Large penmanship

Responsibility: script that is well aligned A an unbiased baseline

Self-confidence A little wide letter with capitals that are well-developed

Sensitivity: unique styles

Sensuality: highly developed lower zone

Spirituality: Developed upper zone However, not extremely wide or tall.

Tolerance: wide forms

Versatility: few angular forms

Chapter 2: Breath Of Personality Science

Klara Roman (1968/1980, in p. 30) defined grapology as being a subset of psychography. William Stern (1900) distinguished between the two methods of variation research--i.e. statistical correlation, as well as techniques of psychography (cited by Lamiell 2003) In which the research focused on a single character among a variety of people and psychography research looked at various traits in one individual.

The distinction between the nomothetic psychology, which studies the generalized aspects of mind and the idiographic sciences of character, which studies the specific constitution of an individual (which is the basis for the study of graphology) is traced to J.S. Mill's A System of Logic (1843/1872) Book VI: The moral sciences' logic.

There are common threads that are common to both graphology and psychology. They both have an extensive history and a brief history. Both trace the origins for their scientific method back to the 1870s. Both are in a battle with the empiricism (quantitative) and intuition (qualitative) ways of investigating the individual.

The two extremes of this conflict are portrayed by positive psychology, as illustrated by Watson's behaviorism on one side and intuitive graphology, as illustrated by Klages"Charakterkunde," or character studies of expressive movement however. Both psychologies were evident in the years following 1910 (Watson 1912, 1914; cited in Allport & Vernon, 1933; Klages, 1910, mentioned in Klages 1932,).

Psychology was established in 1879.

The birth to modern psychological research is generally established in the 1870's following Wilhelm Wundt's research, Principles of physiological psychology, 1873, and the establishment of a laboratory for psychology in 1879. Franz Brentano immediately argued in his Psychology from an empirical point of view 1874, arguing against Wundt's experimentation in psychology and in favor of an practical method (Hellemans and Bunch 1988, p.347).

Carl Stumpf, Edmund Husserl's instructor In the book Psychology of Tone, 1883 warned against both methods of empirical and experimental research, that relied on the physiological experience or sensations in isolation for the determination of psychological universals. The work was based on the principles of the concept of phenomenology. William James brought together the different philosophies in his practical psychology that was which was released as Principles of Psychology, 1890 and shortly thereafter, he founded an institute for psychology within the United States. The way one approaches in psychology, whether that be through experiments or empirical, phenomenological or practical, the modern field of psychology emerged after the 1870's. The first graphology experiment was in 1871.

Modern handwriting analysis was also introduced in the 1870's because of research conducted by Jean-Hypolyte Michelon (1809-1881). "With Michon the history of graphology began" (Saudek 1926, as quoted in Karohs 1985, p.975).

In the group composed of French Theologians from France, Michon is a priest that initially focused on the theory of the character of handwriting from the 1830's. He was also a researcher in the field of historical paleography (a specialization in archeology that studies handwriting) who utilized empirical techniques to study the physical properties of handwriting. He looked at handwritten handwritten documents kept in monisteries and published research papers on the evolution of styles used in handwriting.

Michon discovered numerous graphic signs, or components in handwriting, and developed an empirical way to compare these with the signs of character (Karohs 1985, page. 975). Michon established the graphological society of scientists and a scientific journal in Paris named, Le Journal de l'Autographe, or The Journal of Autography. The term graphologie was first used at first in 18th November issue of 1871.

Philosophical Origins

Michon initially was a student of the theory of handwriting analysis or autography, alongside Abbe Flandrin, who was part of an elite collection that included French theologians. His thinking was probably inspired by St.Thomas Aquinas's dialectic method, as well as by the soul's philosophy.

Aquinus was a professor in The University of Paris, and played a key role in the development of dialectic questions about the scholasticism. In this method, opposing views of a subject were examined to create more clarity through contrast and synthesising the views. Aquinus translated Aristotle's classic Greek philosophy from Arabian texts and conferred it with Christian significance. Aristotle had combined the concepts of Plato as well as Democritus into classical Empiricism. On one hand, was Plato's idealism that saw abstract concepts as a reality hidden behind an illusion of material. The other there was the materialism of Democritus that saw matter as the sole existence; and even thought as just a form of invisible matter.

Islamic doctors and philosophers over the past 500 years contributed to Aristotles's observations of the world as well as his systematic study. Aquinus translated these ideas and correlated them to Christ's life Christ. Aquinus recognized Christ in Jesus Christ a living metaphor that reflected the contradiction and combination of idealism and materialism.

Acquinus believed that the human being was a fusion of two aspects:

1.) the soul within the physical body was associated with a unique memories and experiences (i.e. identity) and

2.) the spirit within the human body God was associated with universality (i.e. the that is, collective consciousness).

"Resurrection of the human body through Christ confirmed the significance of the physical as the primary event that created the individuality of the individual" (Clark 1989, p.8) Soul was closely linked to the physical which in turn, gave the individuality of one's own personal story.

The fundamental nature of every being is inextricably linked with its unique existence, as it is the formal basis for its existence and functioning. For the human, all his activities stem from and are governed through his rationality (soul). The result of this intimate connection is that the essence of a human being is inferred by the nature of its actions (Seidl 1987, page. 456)

This logic implies that an individual's activities, such as their physical appearance, like handwriting, show their character. As Novalis declared:

The soul's seat is located at the intersection between the inner and external realm (cited by Klages 1932 p.37).

Chapter 3: Form-Level And Qualitative Assessment

Ludwig Klages transformed this view of soul that was based on the physical world (i.e. nature-based movement) and the spirit that is associated with Ideal images (i.e. intellectual shape) by defining his notion of expansion and contraction as two competing conflicts of a human being which were to his the ultimate test of character.

The soul desired release, or freedom through spontaneous and active movement. (In cell biology, movement is a characteristic of living.) And the spirit desired to control or structure by restricting or inhibiting this movement to conform to the mental picture or image of the archetypal ideal shape.

Klages' dynamic graphology is based on the concept of contraction and release in the movement of handwriting, as an antagonistic struggle between soul (movement-life-expansion) and spirit (form-measure-constriction). The quality of release that is high that is reflected in the natural flow or rhythm in handwriting, was described as high-form-level or Formnivo.

Form-level is a crucial factor in determining the ability to interpret personality traits positively or negatively. Klages believed that each aspect of a person's personality could become positive or negative depending on whether the individual was controlled (low forms-level) as well as spontaneous (high forms-level). If the writing displayed an extremely high level of form, then the person's traits are expressed in a positive way.

Modern graphologists since Klages have a different understanding of rhythm. Many graphologists think that the handwriting rhythm to be strong, as opposed to simply release in handwriting. is an equilibrium between release and contraction.

"If we took this logic to its most logical conclusion, then we'd be saying that, as the small handwriting can be an indication that a person is contracting, and the larger one is an indicator of release, the huge handwriting of a manic depression when he is in a high state of happiness could indicate a high degree of formality." (Anthony 1964, p. 2. which is cited in Karohs 1987, page. 981).

However, the euphoric state experienced by manic depression is a psychopathological state of mind and shouldn't be linked to an interpretation that is positive of the individual's character.

Klages added she believed that handwriting's quality handwriting release cannot be measured objectively and must be judged by intuition. The debate between intuition or qualitative approaches and statistical or quantitative approaches persists to this day when it comes to the research of the relationship between handwriting and personality (Karohs 1987, p.988).

Chapter 4: Rival Schools Of Graphology

Graphology was first discovered by Michon who developed methodological methods for comparing the components of handwriting which form letters due to the actual dialectic of will conflict and based on the theories developed of Julius Bahnsen (1867) in Contributions to Characterology (cited by Stern 1938).

The French School: A Trait-Structure Methodology

However, Michon identified a myriad of graphic indicators as distinct characters, they were referred to as signs fixes or traits that are fixed. Based on Karohs, (1985, p.975) He also believed that signs negitifs or any sign not visible in handwriting, was also not present in the character of the individual.

Jules Crépieux-Jamine (1858-1940) is a close pupil of Michon and explained Michon's system and proved Michon's signes negitif system was incorrect. He believed that the absence of an indication in handwriting does not necessarily indicate the absence of the trait that characterizes the character of a person. Crepieux-Jamine revised and reorganized Michon's initial system of traits indicators.

In contrast to Michon's view that one handwriting sign was associated with one particular trait, Crepieux-Jamine created a theory of the resultant for secondary and primary traits. Only the primary traits appear directly in handwriting. Secondary or related characteristics have to be assessed using the combination of primary characteristics. Crepieux-Jamine formulated the trait-structure method which is now recognized by the French schools of graphology. (Karohs, 1985)

"The German School: A Dynamic Approach

Alfred Henze (1814-1883), an ancestor of Michon Henze is regarded as to be the one of the first German systematized graphologist. He proved that handwriting was the "expression of a particular motion pattern controlled by brain" (Schweighofer 1979, p.13). Although he was extremely accurate with his charming handwriting sketches however, he didn't actually create a system and was unable to teach anyone to assess the character of a person based on handwriting (Karohs 1987, p.970).

Albrecht Erlenmeyer (1849-1926) was the first doctor to research pathology and physiology based on handwriting characteristics that he published in Die Schrift, Grundzuege Ihrer Pathologie and Physiologie, published from the year 1879 (cited in Karohs 1985).

In the early 1890's, many German graphologists, psychologists,, and medical doctors were involved in establishing a new method for evaluating personality based on handwriting. A number of journals were launched as well as a society, and research that was interdisciplinary was carried out at various universities.

Wilhelm Langenbruch became the first document examinor to be officially recognized in Germany in 1892. Together with Wilhelm Preyer (1841-1897), who was a professor of physiology they established the journal Die Handschrift, in 1895 in Hamburg, Germany. Preyer insists that handwriting is brain-based writing, which means that any muscle in the body that are used for the writing process, after enough time to repetition, will reveal similar movements. (Karohs, 1985)

The year 1897, in Munich, Germany, Hans Busse established his organization, the German Graphological Society and began publishing the Graphologische Monatschefte (Graphological Monthly Journal) in 1897. Georg Meyer (1869-1917), physician who conducted numerous studies on the relationship between handwriting movements and emotional states that were both normal and pathological and frequent contributing author to the journal. Ludwig Klages (1872-1956) was the assistant editor. Klages was poet and philosopher who synthesized research, ideas, and experiments of doctors, physiologists and graphologists in a single philosophical system of thought called biocentrism. (Karohs, 1985).

In the years following 1910, Klages was able to articulate the dynamic approach that differentiated German graphology, which was a distinct from the stroke-trait method that was characteristic of French graphology. The new approach to dynamic research into graphology in Germany focused on the significance of the writing movement in itself. This was in contrast to the French school, which studied particular patterns, or structures of handwriting as a way of determining the deep pattern of personality traits.

Chapter 5: Graphoanalysis A Stroke-Based Approach

The Graphoanalysis school is described as a sroke-based approach which borrowed many of the traits of The French School and some dynamic concepts of The German school.

Milton Newman Bunker (1892-1961) was the founder of the American Graphoanalysis school of handwriting analysis in 1929. addressed personal concerns he had concerning graphology from both an everyday and popular psychology viewpoint. Bunker did not study master's degree in psychology and did not conduct his research under the supervision of an institution of higher learning, but claimed that he learned on his own, and included the ability to read in foreign languages so that he could comprehend graphology books written by himself that were written German in addition to French.

As a shorthand student, his teachers would always begrudgingly comment on his inability of reproducing the exact strokes of shorthand (Smith and Speer 1977). Later, when he was an instructor of shorthand, he noticed the fact that no one of his students could replicate the short strokes of shorthand precisely the same manner, even using the same style of manual. (Sackheim, 1990). He presented the method he used to verify his claims in this passage from the letter:

"In 1910, I was already an established writer for magazines in the fields where people would write to me. I began to study the style of writing first. A plethora of letters passed through my fingers as I wrote, dictated or otherwise thousands on thousands of people, inciting their emotions or even attempting to provoke their emotions. I made nice comments or even insulting things to provoke reactions. I observed the reactions. I followed the reactions. I finally discovered something that was real and worth considering emotional reaction and the absence of it. I kept a lot of correspondence regarding angles that would not have ever come into my life. I guess I could claim that I wrote a lot of letters to love ones, like to see what the response was. When I spoke, I would do something and get a reaction. This, however, was not the sole purpose of generating reactions.

"I have been in the position when I I thought I was establishing the truth and then discovered an inconsistency that was so certain it could have thrown off my calculations. After that, I would take trains or buses and spend various amounts of time with an person, and talk to those who had intimate knowledge of the person and that's the way I came to an understanding that one character trait could hold an other one back.

Since I was as a co-editor of a family magazine that had an average circulation of 2 million people, I was able to have every aspect of human life to monitor. (Speer Smith and Speer 1977, p.8-9, excerpt from personal letters which was later reprinted)

In 1927, Bunker examined his conclusions that he came at regarding handwriting applying them to hiring and firing decisions made by an organization he was involved with in the past. He compared his choices solely based on handwriting with decisions using references, which was the criteria that the company employed. He tracked his results over a period of at least 18 months, and discovered that his approach "was more effective in attracting employees than what was required of the company" (Speer Smith and Smith 1977, p.9).

In the same letter , which is partially that was mentioned earlier, Bunker wrote that he had no intention of teaching handwriting analysis. However, Bunker "began giving grapho analyses against my will" in 1929 when he created his own organization, the American Institute of Grapho-Analysis, which later became known as the International Graphoanalysis Society in 1949 (Speer Smith and Speer 1977, p.10).

Sackheim 1990, argues that Bunker is not mentioned in the academic texts due to the "folksy way of writing" as well as the fact that Bunker promoted his Graphoanalysis as an MBA institution (p.xvii). Sackheim is of the opinion his "his impact on the discipline was massive," because he combined with his method of studying the handwriting strokes the finest features of both German dynamic graphology and French characteristic graphology (p.xvii).

Some graphologists believe Bunker contributed little towards the discipline. Andrea McNichol, graphologist who was interviewed by Psychology Today editors Scanlon & Mauro in 1992, believes that

Graphoanalysis is an "simplistic branch of graphology" since it grew from popular psychology, rather than as an alternative to the psychiatry field in the university setting, as the case in Europe (p.48).

It is possible to argue that the eclectic approach which graphologists use in their work (Nevo 1986, page. 777) usually draws from both the trait and dynamic graphology of the two primary systems, including Bunker's Graphoanalysis approach. Bunker however does not provide specific reference to research conducted in either French nor the Germans schools.

Bunker justified his attitude towards research in a private letter (1955):
One final observation I'd like to add to the research. I have witnessed members of the [International GraphoanalysisSociety] claim to be conducting research. The pretense, and this is the case with every handwriting study conducted in the United States, was laid in the hope of proving some thing. I wasn't looking to prove anything. I was just looking for results. The majority of this information disappeared years ago, because I wasn't

trying in order to demonstrate something for anyone or anyone else. I set out to find my own personal answers. I received the answers. (Speer & Smith, 1977, p. 10).
American Psychologists" Attitude

Allport as well as Vernon (1932) Vernon (1932) used an academic approach to make graphology accepted for psychologists in Harvard along with other American universities, had a limited impact. Allport's graphology-related research interests was triggered by the publication of his paper which focused on Klages the concept of the form-level concept The Undivided Personality (Allport 1924) after a visit to William Stern in Germany. Allport and Vernon's 1932, scientific research into how expressive movements that was a result of dynamic graphology However, it also contained a review of the validity of research on graphology.
In the same year, an international journal of graphology research established itself as the leading journal throughout the United States (Character and Personality 1932) and graphology was completely neglected from American psychologists.

However Bunker's approach to graphology was low-brow. helped to make graphology more acceptable to people of all ages. He made graphology more simple and easy to comprehend, meaning that anyone who lives at home could join the opportunity to study in the comfort of her living room. The correspondence school has graduated more than 40,000 students, which makes Graphoanalysis the most widely-known method of analysis of hadwriting in America. This is the contradiction between academic psychology destain of psychologists and the general lowbrow fascination for analysis of handwriting across North America.

Chapter 6: Experimental Graphology

INTERGRATIVE Approach

Robert Saudek (1881-1935) wanted to bring together the French and German school of graphology by employing methods of experiential psychology. He also created the graphology journal Character and Personality in 1932.

Saudek carried out precise experiments regarding handwriting movement and its connection to the characteristics of personality by using psychological statistics. He used photography and microscope analysis and also lab instruments he created himself to carry out extremely precise physical measurements of handwriting motion particularly in relation to the speed of writing.

His principal conclusion is that speed at which he wrote was the primary factor that influenced any other physical expressions in handwriting and that the natural speed of the handwriting of the person was vital to determine for a precise handwriting analysis.

As natural as the writing is, the more fully the writer's personality is revealed. Unnaturally fast speed for the writer would indicate artificial and fake handwriting which could conceal more of the character of the writer than it revealed. Saudek published the results of his research over 26 years through The Psychology of Handwriting, 1926 (cited in Karohs 1985) as well as Experiments with Handwriting, 1929.

Experiments were conducted with the handwritings of more than 100,000 people: including women, men and children from diverse nationalities and classes and with those who practice different writing styles that are left-handed or right-handed as well as short-sighted and long-sighted as well as those who suffer from partial or permanent impairment or temporary, of the muscle system of the arm or hand. People who have a tendency to write with exuberant writing styles have been forced to write as slack as they can, and people who usually use with a smaller, simpler hand have attempted to write using big and powerful strokes. (Brooks 1950, p.9, cited in Karoh's 1985, p. 1999)

The experiments of Saudek were important because they utilized more rigorously controlled and precise, measurements that were based on the ethos of British empiricists,

99

and applying modern methods of statistical analysis favored by Thorndike. Georg Meyer also had conducted systematic studies focusing on the relation between emotions and writing movements and the challenge of changing different handwriting indicators on the fly He published these findings his findings in The Scientific Foundations of Graphology in the year 1901 (cited in Karohs 1985). Meyer's research was developed from a medical point of view.

Gordon W. Allport and Philip E. Vernon summarized the state of graphology experimental in the publication Studies in Expressive Movement (1933) and also included a thorough review of the literature (see Powers, 1933). Allport and Vernon, 1933 they praised the work of Saudek as the most exemplary examples of experimental methods in graphology. They concluded with a sarcastic statement that:
"Curiously enough Saudek is attacked in Germany as being too statistically-minded, and in America for his 'vague speculation'." (p.189).

Allport & Vernon commented that J.B. Watson's comment reflected the general view of distrust and doubt towards graphology within American psychologists. Watson stated that in Psychology from the viewpoint of a behaviorist in 1919 and that

the one experiment by Hall and Montgomery in 1919 proved "that every graphology claim are just a matter of exaggerations that are not able to stand rigorous experimental testing'"(cited in Allport & Vernon, 1933, p.185).

Allport and Vernon refer to Werner Wolff's assertion about this methodological issue in character research:

This is the standpoint of characterology today: Either we have followers of the statistical-mechanical procedure which yields a crude succession of single elements which never give a living picture; or else we have the intuitive penetration which, it is true, can delineate brilliantly the living processes of human beings, but cannot be communicated, verified, or utilized for a knowledge of genetic relationships (cited in Allport & Vernon, 1933, p. 11).

Allport and Vernon 1933, attempted to find a middle way between these two issues and the theoretical question in the following manner:

"Unless we believe in the epistemology of intuitionism we must consider our personal judgments as inferential concepts based on our perceptions of the world around us and assume that it is solely by our perceptions of our bodies' physical appearance or the gestures, speech, or words of our friends that we can gain any understanding of their characteristics. From this perspective, the study of expression directly can be the best method to study personality"(p.v).

The tests carried out by Allport and Vernon in 1933, although initially, were merely preliminary and were aimed at establishing the consistency (i.e. the reliability) of a person's diverse expressive actions known as expressive movements. This credibility needed for it to be proven before reliability of determining the connection between the peculiarities in expression as well as the personality's inner dispositions could be accurately identified.

Allport and Vernon 1933, who cite the graphology research conducted from

American psychologist Downing 1919, as the closest to their own study of the consistency of expressive movements.

"The discovery of well-integrated , constant expression within the motor domain would make it clear that similar patterns can be expected across every aspect of the personality, however it will be an ongoing task to establish how expressive movements to inner characteristics as well as to impressions" (Allport and Vernon 1933, p. VIII)

The two researchers were hoping that the most prestigious journal of research about Character and Personality, with simultaneous publication in Munich, London and Durham, North Carolina (at Duke University in the USA) could help to focus future research on this subject and solve these issues in the methodology (Allport and Vernon 1933, p.186, footnote).

Chapter 7: What Happened To Graphology?

Experimental graphology has provided a lot of inspiration for improvement in measurements, statistics, as well as instruments for the field of psychological assessment. Handwriting analysis is also connected to the development of research into psychology in general as expressed in different theories of thought, including deep psychology, gestalt psychoanalysis, analytic psyhology, and psychological anthropology, aswell medical psychiatry as well.

From 1926 onwards, in an London gathering at the British Psychological Society, Robert Saudek presented a hefty collection of research in psychographics for the Medical Psychology Section (Saudek, 1927, as cited by Nigel in 2005).

In the United States, A.A. Roback was a professor of the field of experimental graphology in Harvard University. He also directed research projects and held academic conferences in the emerging area of graphology that is experimental (Gerber 1936). In a 1931 overview of study, the researcher emphasized

"interest for the topic, in particular in Europe is growing quickly, and the production of new literature is fascinating both in its sheer volume and the level of quality" (cited in Allport & Vernon, 1933, p.185, footnote:1).

Robert Heiss (1903-1974), philosopher and physiologist who related ideas of depth psychology and graphological manifestations of space, movement and form. Werner Wolff, 1943, utilized the ideas of depth psychology and summarized research carried out on determining the the consistency of expressive movement that Allport and Vernon in 1933 considered essential to the confirmation of graphology. Then Wolff in 1948, utilized the ideas of depth psychology in experiments for graphology Diagrams of the Unconscious: handwriting and personality as measured in as well as analysis and experiment.

Schweighofer (1979 in 1979, page. 15.) believed that the subsequent experiments were the most comprehensive confirmation of graphology prior to the 1930s, and could have been the first step towards scientific acceptance for graphology.

(1) Arnheim (1928) and Theiss (1931) research in graphology in Gestalt theory [also mentioned in Allport and Vernon in 1933, p.186].

(2) Johannes Rudert's long-running studies on graphic indicators graphology, at the Psychological Institute of the University of Leipzig, Germany in the late 1930s .

The majority of the work was never translated into English and at the close of the decade, much of research as well as communications taking place in this area was dispersed and tangled due to the rising of Nazism and World War II so that publication was either stopped or was delayed for a lot of psychologists.

Unfortunate events in 1935

Tragically, Robert Saudek died in 1935 from an undiagnosed ailment, just a few years after he founded the graphology experimental journal in 1932, which was dubbed Character and Personality. Duke University in Durham, North Carolina, then bought this international journal for research in graphology from the widow of Robert Saudek, and then changed Character and Personality into the first scientific journal focusing that focused on psychometric personality tests.

The long list of collaborators who were interested in graphology research, such as Carl Jung, Alfred Adler and Gordon Allport, were soon replaced by an editorial board comprised only of personality test psychologists. At the close year, the war with Germany affected any contact between the continental European and English psychologists who spoke English.

In Germany in the wake of the nazifacation and training in psychology in the country, the Fortune Telling Law was issued by the Berlin police chief in 1935, which banned any graphology, with the exception of Klages"intuitive graphology.

The statute "enabled the Klages's group to defame 80-90 percent of all graphologists, and to cut off their incomes" (Otto Junge 1949, as quoted in Karohs 1985, Page. 987).

Psychologist Otto Junge had been preparing to publish his book on Rationale Graphology. Though it was based on the same theories to Klages', like expansion and contraction as opposing tendencies the book was later censored because he assigned quatitative scores to the respective tendencies in the handwriting (Karohs 1985, p.985).

Unfortunately, Otto Junge was not able to publish his book until 4 years after the end of the war in 1949. However, at the time, a prominent graphological journal slammed Rational Graphology because the journal editors believed it was a statistics to the detriment of instruction. This is why Rational Graphology did not become extremely well-known in Germany.

Thea Stein Lewinson (1986) in collaboration with Dr. Joseph Zubin, further developed this objective scale to statistically measure rhythm in handwriting based on Klages' contraction-and-release concept. But whereas Klages saw rhythm as a sign of release, the Lewinson-Zubin scale considered rhythm to be a balanced norm between contraction-and-release. Based on the Otto Junge's (1949) Rational Graphology principles of objective measurement as well as Lewinson (1986), Erika Karohs created The Graphodiagnostic System of Handwriting Analysis 1988.

Karohs graphodiagnostic system assigns equal weighting in quantitative for each handwriting component of her comprehensive five-volume manual including interpretations of statistical scores (Clayton

1991, p.5). Karohs graphodiagnostic System is built on the following principles:

(1) Klages' contraction/release theory, was developed in the work of Lewinson as well as Zubin,

(2) The depth theory of Pulver as the unconscious exeression of the writer's physical and psychic energy as well as

(3) Saudek's concepts of speed of writing to help in understanding other data related to handwriting. (The Graphodiagnostic System is reviewed by Karohs 1989 and Clayton, 1991.)

Access to English to the work of Otto J. Junge and other graphology research is accessible in the present mainly due to Erika Karoh's translations. She also collated, edited and indexed a lot of the data which she translated and put into a 30 volume Handbook for Handwriting Analysts. Through her translations, she provided detailed citations of the French in addition to German research literatures to give historical context.

Chapter 8: The Advancement Of Clinical Graphology

Clinical graphology refers to the application of projection techniques to the examination of handwriting in the context of psychotherapy and critical psychiatry. This consultation discipline based assessments of individual apraisal on an inter-disciplinary body of research that is peer reviewed in journals of the human sciences rather than limiting the research and practice of individual apraisal only to a specific school of psychology.

In the 1930s, in the 1930s at Sorbonne In Paris The use of graphology in psychotherapy was investigated in clinical trials conducted by psychotherapist Peirre Janet, who was a professor of psychiatry in the College de France (Seifer, 2009, p.42; Ellenberger, 1970, p.346). At the close in World War II, Janet's protégé Paul de Sainte Colombe along with a host of psychotherapists had emigrated to America.

A majority of European psychotherapists received training in graphology and helped in expanding the knowledge base of graphology in clinical practice. For instance, graphology is a term used in the Longman Dictionary of Psychology and Psychiatry describes graphology as

The study of the pattern and physical properties of writing, as a method to identify the writer and indicating his mental state prior to writing, or to evaluate the characteristics of his personality (R. M. Golden PhD Editor in Chief 1984, page. 324).

Paul de Sainte Colombe taught the methods of projective clinical graphology that aid in diagnosing both mental and physical health throughout the United States. His teacher, Pierre Janet had been the pioneer of the concept of psychological analysis as well as the theory of dissociation within the field of depth psychology (from his initial research about the unconscious dynamic from the earlier century prior to Freud and Jung).

Janet's theory of psychological dissociation was essential for the concept of Carl Jung of dominant and inferior functions, like the ability to sense-intuit and feel-think. Freud's theory of repression with a particular focus on the sex drive that is repressed as libido, on the other of the other hand, was the principal theory Freud used to explain the psychoanalysis of deams (Ellenberger 1970).

Schweighofer, 1979, employed graphology to study psychoanalysis's psychohistory from writings of Sigmund Freud, as well as the circle of his. Psychoanalysis (Sigmond Freud) and analytical psychology (Carl Jung) were derived from the psychological analysis of Pierre Janet's method (Ellenberger 1970).

It is believed that the Swiss psychotherapist Max Pulver was also a founding member of the Analytical Psychology Association with Carl Jung. He recognized an psychodynamic representation of symbolic meaning in space as a key element to the assessment of handwriting projection in the field of clinical graphology. Max Pulver and Carl Jung were acquainted at Burgholzli the psychiatric institution managed by Eugen Bleuler in Zurich, Switzerland, where they both worked at the start of their careers.

Psychotherapists from the Analytical Psychology Association in Switzerland they were influenced by one another throughout their professional lives. The other person who was Influenced from Max Pulver was analytical psychologist Ania Teillard, who was a student of Jung for more than 30 years. She applied Carl Jung's four main functions (sensation-intuition and feeling-thinking) to graphology, together with the two attitudes (introvert-extrovert), the two tendencies: (animus-anima) and the persona.

Analytical psychology research conducted by Ania Teillard at the C.G. Jung Institute in

Zurich motivated her to merge graphology and analytical psychology. She studied graphology under Ludwig Klages, as well as Jules Crepieux-Jamin , and Robert Saudek. Following after the First World War, Saudek was a lecturer at various universities throughout Europe in graphology experiments and graphology, including Amsterdam and influenced the advancement of academic programs through creating The scientific journal published by the graphologists' professional society in the Netherlands that is still published to this day (Bradley 2005).

Dr. Graumann was studying the methods of graphology in the clinic in the purposes of his Ph.D course in psychotherapy within the Neatherlands before moving into Topeka, Kansas where I met Dr. Graumann at the Menninger Clinic. The doctor used graphology in clinical settings in his psychiatric therapy and also for assessments of the doctoral students within Menninger Clinic. Menninger Clinic. Graumann 1983, who was a major influencer, sparked the author's interest in clinical graphology while they were at the Menninger Clinic at that time was located in Topeka, Kansas.

POST SCRIPT - on Postmodern Graphology

Handwriting analysis, also known as graphology, is the study of physical features of handwriting in order to determine the patterns of repetitive movements in ink the inner dynamics of the individual's character. The writer is assessed in general terms by looking at the patterns of automatic movement in their handwriting, which is believed as an (unconscious) expression of their psychodynamic character. The evaluation of character with graphology does not constitute a trait of personality test, but rather a deep psychological test that is projective.

The empirical studies of critical psychiatry have confirmed the validity of character evaluation with graphology (Cronje and Roets 2013) But those who advocate for fixed test theory for personality assert that studies do not demonstrate that there is scientific proof that graphology is valid (Coon and Mitterer 2009). Skeptics have exaggerated numerous low correlations between personality traits by using the classical test theory methods for test of personality traits to argue that graphology is not a reliable personality test.

Psychologists who believe that graphology is an instrument for psychometric testing (Meir & Bar-Hillel, 1986) or ought to be (Bar-Hillel and Ben-Shakhar, 1986) are unable to accept the value that graphology is a psychometric test. In the vanity media of the Skepticism movement particularly as demonstrated through Dean (1992) Fanatics from a skeptical scientific perspective employ simple manipulations of statistics for their bully pulpit take on and discredit graphologists.

Professional courage is necessary to dig deeper into the bogus science to determine the legitimacy of graphology on your own. While the debate over graphology's validity has raged on throughout the last century, the skeptical organizations that dominate online platforms keep reputations in the dark in every debate about graphology's validity.

Unfortunately, personality psychology is an incredibly controversial sciencethat Hogan in 1987 described for being "a source of a vague embarrassment for the field" (p.80). The bad actors therefore have the opportunity to benefit from the associations for personality psychology and peer-reviewed journals. Most anti-graphology fans aren't even psychologists (such as Dean 1992). Journalists and editors associated with the skepticism skeptics movement have infiltrated the internet and forums, but not to debate legitimately on the validity of graphology but to hold professional reputations in the hands of a few.

The absence of statistical relationship between handwriting and personality has not invalidated graphology. However the concept of a trait-based theory of personality is discredited when contrasted with graphological assessments which are primarily clinical. In contrast to the reductionism idea of traits that define personality holism notion of character is not able to be divided into distinct parts that can be compared with other people, when graphology is built in theories about functional integration for the entire individual. Consider handwriting as a form of expression (Micale 2014, 187-88) The concept of graphology hasn't been disproved by the absence of correlation between handwriting traits and personality characteristics.

Instead of looking at the overall function of personality from the viewpoint from a point of view, the personality test examine the amount of statistically significant characteristics of a person when compared with the population by using psychological measurement theory , which is also known as nonparametric statistical correlation , which is derived from an reductionist perspective of the traditional test theory, also that is known as nomothetic analysis of personality characteristics.

There are some bad actors within the billion-dollar business of personality tests view graphologists as rivals. There are many factors that prevent clinical graphologists from taking over even a small portion of the mass produced products within the market for personality tests. The qualitative aspects of assessment are not entirely automated. Similar to any psychotherapy assessment clinical graphology demands an individualized approach to the ethical evaluation of an individual, however the individual does not have to be present for the exam or a written examination.

Clinical graphologists are in a limited numbers and the process of evaluating them hinders them from participating with the automated mass test of personality. The ability to evaluate physical characteristics of handwriting is a process that requires an apprentice phase along with specialist education that limits the number of graphologists in clinical. To ensure accuracy in measurement clinical graphologists need the original handwritten documents to examine physically.

The test makers may be concerned that the graphological method of individual appraisal could jeopardize their credibility as a scientific method for tests for personality. However, the knowledge of individual dynamics that clinical graphology can provide through the assessment of handwriting projection is not going to replace the kind of predictions on correlation that rigorously assessed psychometric tests can offer.

What's at odds in the battle between personality testing and clinical graphology are two extremes in the idiographic and nomothetic perspectives which aren't to be in a position to be to be reconciled. Similar to the charioteer of classical times that was described by Greek philosopher Plato The author has the impression like he's in the midst of two horses which are constantly fighting against each against each other.

One horse is black with control, but no energy or enthusiasm to keep moving towards the goal rather, it drags downwards, steadily toward the ground. The other horse is an white horse that is full of energy, but has not enough control to maintain an even pace, and is a jerk toward the sun! If both horses were able to join together and harness their respective most desirable qualities, the job could become a blend of their best qualities.

In the meantime, until the inner and outer perspectives are able to be co-ordinated the expert who is using clinical graphology will have to navigate the numerous idiographic and nomothetic oppositions of both sciences. The long-running dispute between graphology and psychometry is not going to be solved by trying to integrate clinical graphology within the framework of testing for personality traits regardless of whether it is conducted as a critical psychiatrist support of, and as an uncritical scientist in opposition to an assessment of handwriting that is projective.

If the differences between personality tests and graphology are recognized and acknowledged, the two opposing approaches to assessing personality are in reality complementary to one another. The most reliable personality tests can reveal the way a person's personality appears relative to other people and clinical graphology provides an in-depth and accurate view of the inner structure of a person's personality.

Chapter 9: Determinism Vs Free Will

The core of this debate between graphology and psychology is the issue of how much freedom is available to influence the development of one's self as person, versus how much of one's development and development is determined by external factors as well as genetic inheritance. The freedom of choice is associated with graphology and character science while determinism is linked to personality psychology through psychometric personality test.

The more freedom one enjoys in their individual development, the more subjective the measures are for making predictions about what the person will be able to do. Klages believed that psychologists' quest for universal law was in fact, what hindered an empirical recognition of a person based on the facts that are their own expression.

Charles Darwin (1809-1882), when accumulating his wealth of information on evolution, noticed that his handwriting resembled similar to the grandfather's (Erasmus Darwin) handwriting. Charles said that their interests and personalities were identical. On the 6th of January 1839 He wrote in his notebook:

The handwriting of a person is determined through the most complicated conditions, as evidenced by the difficulty of forging, and yet handwriting is said to be inherited. It reveals [sic.how the smallest details of hereditary structure. (Darwin, 1987, p.420)

Darwin published a short outline of his thoughts On the Origin of Species by means of Natural Selection in 1859. Following that, he released several other works on psychology, including The Expression of emotions of Man and Animals 1872, that greatly influenced the study human behavior from the standpoint of physical determination. (Cited in Clark 1989)

Charles Darwin's cousin Sir Francis Galton (1822-1911), was extremely interested in the assessment of differences between individuals to establish that human intelligence was passed down through the generations. Galton pioneered statistical techniques that could be used to measure both mental and genetics. He established the use of questionnaires to assess psychological intelligence which were a method for personality tests. These were that were published in Measurement of character (Galton, 1884).

Galton invented the first method for assessing idea-association and word-association that led to the psychoanalysis-based projective test, also known as the word association test, which was developed more thoroughly through Carl Jung (leading to free association tests and structured ones).

Galton discovered in "experiments intended to establish whether people could actually freely decide what thoughts they would like to think in their minds," according to Gregory Galton, 1987, that the free will did not have anything to play in it (p. 283.).

A. American psychotherapist, Edward Thorndike (1874-1949) was profoundly affected by Galton. Thorndike (1904) created methods for turning results from qualitative research into analysis in his book An Introduction to the Theory of Mental and Social Measurements. Even fields that are not as distinct, such as the fields of experimental psychology and social psychology today are based on the same principles laid in Thorndike (1904) with his textbook that was influential for research and analysis of data from psychology.

Thorndike 1915b used these statistical techniques to Galton's issue of intellectual inheritance and the resemblance of Young Twins in Handwriting. Thorndike also conducted extensive research on handwriting in the field of education to come up with a more precise method of evaluating the handwriting quality (Thorndike 1915a).

Chapter 10: Persona

Every handwriting style is unique. A person's script is an expression of who they are as well as their innermost thoughts, emotions as well as the desires of his or her subconscious. Though a pencil or pen is held in the palm of your hand at the end of the day writing is controlled by the organ that defines the uniqueness of every person's brain.

This is the basis of the art of handwriting analysis. This is the reason why it can be used to determine the traits of a person's behavior and temperament.

To begin to discover the secrets of your personality through handwriting, it is necessary to start by preparing a few things.

The Specimen

This is the handwriting sample that is used in analysis. The handwriting sample should be written in paragraphs as much as is possible. The paper used must be completely blank, with no gridlines or any imposed margins. This limits the creative freedom of the writer, and creates a paper that isn't fully reflective of their style of writing.

It is essential to get an image that is as natural as is possible. The handwriting of the author must reflect the authentic, natural style. A style that is mechanical or acquired does not offer enough distinctiveness for an analysis to be based on.

A manual for handwriting (no matter how big) is not a better alternative to a standard notebook. The reason is that reproducing the letters exactly as they appear in a book for exercise takes away much of the originality and uniqueness which is essential to handwriting analysis.

Certain people are able to have multiple writing style.

The Materials

Although your eyes and brain are the most important tools to analyze handwriting Other tools will assist you in improving not only the outcome of your analysis, but also the process of it, too.

A magnifying glass can be a useful tool to have in your arsenal. Reading for long periods of time is enough of a strain for the eyes already without taking into consideration the great focus on detail that is typical. This can aid in identifying subtle differences that might be missed through a simple examination with your eyes alone.

A protractor is essential to determine the slant of the letters. This is a crucial aspect in handwriting analysis. A ruler is employed to determine the distance between margins as well as the height of letters, which is a vital aspect of the art of graphology. The significance of these elements will be explored deeper in the future.

Once you have a better understanding of what makes a quality handwriting sample and the essential tools and materials required for a successful handwriting experiment, you're now ready to embark on your first journey into graphology!

There are a myriad of characteristics to consider when looking at the handwriting of an individual. Every nuances of a handwriting will help you identify the characteristics that define the character of a person.

Here are some things to be aware of when conducting a handwriting analysis to find the character of a person:

It is the Slope of Letters

The slope, sometimes referred to as slant, in handwriting is one of the most obvious indicators of temperament.

Writing that is heavily slanted towards the right is a characteristic of those who are emotional compassionate, sympathetic, and sentimental. They are artistic and creative and often possess a strong affinity to music, poetry, art as well as other pursuits of creativity. They are committed to both those who are dear to them as well as the mission to which they have dedicated their lives for.

A sharp slant to the left isn't nearly so common as one that is that is to the right. The person who has this style of writing can be seen retreating and not expressing emotions. They could also adopt an "what's to be gained from this?" kind of stance in all situations.

The slope or slant may be affected by the writer's mental state during the process of writing. The stronger the slant, the more intense the emotion associated with the phrase or word.

If the slope is different from left to right in the same sentence it could indicate an individual's difficult or inability to make decisions. It could indicate an imbalance between the person's "head" as well as "heart" or so to put it in a nutshell. A person with this type of personality is likely to withdraw emotionally and introverted when they are feeling anxious. The erratic mood swings can be noticed.

The Integrity of Letters

As slant and slope suggests certain characteristics, the complete absence of it can be a sign of other characteristics as well.

Vertical and upright letters suggest that one is driven more by logic judgement and reasoning than emotions, imagination or impulsiveness. They are usually independent practical and can seem uninterested or cold at times.

The authors who use a straight script are drawn to rational activities, not romantic and artistic pursuits. People who are dedicated to the pursuit of mathematical and scientific knowledge generally choose this kind of writing.

It is the Angularity of Letters

An angular handwriting style is a signpost for those who are proactive and determined in their search for success. Writers with precise lines and clear angles tend to be very motivated in their pursuit of success. They may not be naturally inclined to be successful however, they will try the best they can to get it.

They can also be very careful and precise when it comes to their assessment of others and themselves. Because of this, people view them as rough rigid, aggressive, and even stern. But when paired with the hand that is sloping and angularity, it indicates that the writer has a view of emotions and sentimentality in his judgement too.

A Roundedness in Letters

Contrasting with round letters, angular letters are typical for people who have a positive temperament. They are usually calm and peaceful. They are averse to conflict and will try to avoid conflict if they have the opportunity. Agression is not their nature.

Writers with rounded scripts are also extremely flexible. They are happy with their current situation and what they have. They're also usually contemplative about the current state of their lives.

If the script doesn't have any angular or angular form, it might suggest a person is a bit too at ease and has an "go along with what's happening" approach that can result in a very unfocused life.

Writing Tracings of Letters

Tracing is the way one writes letters, regardless of whether they hold their pen securely and lightly, heavily or in a weak way, and so on.

A firm tracing is a clear indicator of a healthy body. It is also a sign of determination, motivation and determination.

The weak tracing indicates that the writer's mental or physical health is in decline. It could be an indication of extreme shyness.

The heavy tracing could be a sign of materialistic tendencies. People who are a bit heavy handed with writing tend to be enthralled by the finest things in life. They are drawn to luxury and elegance.

The trace of light is a sign of a strong religious conviction. The ethical and aesthetic aspects influence the thinking of these writers than physical things.

Rapid tracing can be a sign of mental stimulation and energy. It can be the result of excitement that is expressed through larger uppercase letters, and frequent downward strokes. It could be a result of anger, which can result in extremely sharp angles as well as extended crosses of lowercase "t".

The legibility and inability of Letters

The more accessible a written piece is more likely the writer to display an honest, open and honest character. People who are like this tend to be clear in their communication and want to be treated with respect. This is particularly evident when paired with an the angular shape and strong tracing.

Ink that is unclear could signal the writer's intention to conceal what is being written. This could be an indication of a shady nature.

It could also be a result of a mind that's quick to think or draw conclusions and causes the hand to be unable to keeping up. This is the situation with many talented writers, professors or scientists with handwritten notes that are frequently unreadable to anyone other than their own.

The Regularity and irregularity of Letters

In this instance, the term "regularity" refers to how consistently every letter written. Are the handwriting and handwriting uniform? Do the letter "I" and "the" appear identical to other letters? Are there any subtle differences that can be noticed?

The regularity of handwriting could indicate the consistency of a person's personality. Writers with consistent formats for their letters are likely to have a consistent style of behaviour. If they're non-aggressive and peaceful They will stay the same in all situations. However, if they're determined and not afraid of confrontation, they will show this throughout their relationships.

In the end, they tend to react in a predictable way to situations given to them.

The term "irregular" refers to letters that aren't uniform or consistent can mean a variety of things.

When paired with a distinct right-sided slope and a strong tracery, this could suggest an individual who is often emotional, spontaneous, indecisive and lively in their the world of. But, when it is paired with the weakest tracing or roundness, it could be a sign of a shaky and uncertain character.

The Compression of Letters

Writing letters may be done in condensed or in a more extended way.

The extent of compression could be related to the level of thriftiness. A moderately compressed text is an indication of practical prudence and the ability to cut costs and save money, whereas an extreme compression could be a sign of a severe miserly lifestyle motivated by greed.

However writing letters that aren't compressed indicates that the person is generous in their nature. If handwriting is lengthy by a couple of words per line, the writer is generally friendly and social with a broad perspective.

The Pretentiousness and Simplicity of Letters

Simple scripts are ones that does not have extravagant flourishes or ornaments.

People who have simple, small and sluggish handwriting are usually humble and modest. They are modest and grounded. People with simple, yet large and wide handwriting, are more confident in their self-esteem as well as pride however, they aren't overt in their display of confidence. They typically have a calm manner of speaking that commands respect.

What is opposite to a basic script is a pretentious one. The most lavishly decorated and adorned letters fall into this category. Handwriting like this conveys self-confidence , which often borders on arrogance, particularly if there is no style or elegance to the writing. Individuals who make their handwriting excessively ornamental are susceptible to self-esteem and self-importance.

It is possible to confuse this with the imaginative handwriting of an artist, however their handwriting as people are the product of imagination or spontaneity. It is not the result intentional pretension.

The Letters' Size Letters

In general, big letters can be a sign of pride. The writer's pride may be based on many aspects, like their values of courage, dignity, or a healthy feeling of self-esteem. But, if large letters are combined with an overtly extravagant style, it could be a sign of superficial pride, which is more concerned with the appearance of oneself than actually feeling proud of oneself.

Small letters signify an intelligent and scholarly mind. A person who is humble and sensitive is an appropriate description for the author of a short and simple script.

A Separation and Connectedness Letters

Connected letters represent an unrestricted thought process with an mind that is typically analytical, logical, and adept in the synthesis of ideas. The people who write this way tend to be opinionated and enjoy the thrill of discussion. They can make solid decisions based on facts and reasoning. Their ability to defend and make an argument in a clear manner is their forte.

While separated letters are a sign of an individual with a good sense. They make their decisions quickly, yet they still display amazing fluency when communicating their ideas. Their persuasive skills are not so much based on the facts, but in their passionate and persuasive presentation.

the Ascent and Descent of Lines and Letters

Together with an angular and strong style, the ascending lines and letters convey a determined and affluent personality. Handwriting of this type is common among people who want to succeed. They aim to rise higher than the average in all aspects and their writing style shows this.

Descending lines and letters in contrast can be a signal of hopelessness and depression in particular if they are not accompanied by angularity or strong trace. This is a handwriting of someone who experienced--or is experiencing--adversity, but who lacks the strength to combat it. It is a popular way to express feelings of being betrayed and depressed.

The Punctuation

Punctuation marks that are carefully placed can be a sign of a tidy and diligent person who pays close focus on the small details. However when they're not placed in the correct place or absent altogether, this could be an indication of mental disorder.

With these characters to keep an eye for, you will discover the character of someone by their writing!

But remember that characteristics uncovered through analysis should be evaluated as a whole, and not as distinct elements. If the personality of a person is painted that is painted by individual characteristics, then these are the strokes that comprise the painting. To understand the entire image, it is essential to examine how the aspects interact and also how they are a part of the whole.

This will enable you to make an accurate and precise analysis.

Writing a slant

In essence, there are three major directions that the slants of the writing will point to since people usually have a primary direction the direction that their letters slant but a written piece may contain a mix of the various slant directions. The slant directions include:

Right

Vertical

Left

The three directions in these three directions represent three distinct characteristics of people. The right slant direction can be interpreted to show an emotional and expressive nature that writers possess. Vertical slants typically indicate the ability to calculate of the writer. A left-hand slant signifies an indecisiveness or a lack of confidence.

The various slants just as the right slant depicts the person who is truly extroverted and more friendly. If we look at human personality traits and personalities, we will see that these people fall within the choleric and sanguine temperament. They are known to be extremely social and social, and they are quick to strike up conversations with strangers. Certain books on temperaments make mention of this group of people who might have difficulty keeping secrets due to their sociable nature. Therefore, the nature of these traits can help handwriting analysts who are looking for information about negative or positive instances.

The vertical slant that is mentioned is a concern for those who are more analytical and seek to manage issues in a responsible manner, recognizing the desire to remain completely impartial. Analysts may find these individuals useful, particularly when making recommendations for positions that require analysis and less social or human interactions. These people may be more independent when contrasted to their colleagues or colleagues. A complete belief in their ability to reach their goals with no or little assistance is a characteristic displayed by these people.

Left-slant writers are people who are shy and may be reluctant to make decision. People who are introverted may be less adept at their social interaction analysts might find them useful in positions that require only human interaction. However, their ability to handle particulars is an asset for them, and any place they are employed.

THE PRESSURE

The pressure that is applied when writing tells a lot more than can be known about a person those who apply a great pressure while writing create the impression of being tight A little force can indicate seriousness, while light force suggests an sensitivity to the people around them and also the environment. The force applied is evident in the use of ink on the paper, which is typically darker. The feel underneath the paper tells a lot about the force applied while writing.

Writing with low pressure or inconsistent pressure may indicate a lack of enthusiasm for a writer. An appropriate step should be taken for such a person to avoid being considered to be inactive. They are not too receptive to any challenge, although silent aggression may be an occurrence among them.

SCREENING ZONE

The writing zone is all with how high or low the strokes that writers go. An examination of the patterns of writing of certain individuals shows their enthusiasm for exaggerating the lengths of letters like the capital letter 'L' or by extending to the smaller letter "t upwards. Thus, the lengthening of these letters upwards is considered to be an upper-level zone. The use of longer strokes downward is referred to as the lower or downward zone.

Upper zone

This group of writers is well-known for showing the necessity of achieving their goals and objectives. They want to stand out from the crowd and be noticed. Their expectations could go over the bounds of reasonable expectations, particularly with bizarre lower strokes writers.

However, the capacity for imagination of writers who write in upper strokes is useful in situations where it is necessary to have this skill. Also, projects that need to meet difficult deadlines could be an ideal opportunity for those who fall into this category.

Upper zone writers may be classified further into Heavy pressure and light pressure writers. The upper pressure writers are more active or responsive at any time and are able to take decisions without having to consult prior. Their actions can be compared to those who are at the front lines of war that consider their lives more important than having to conduct consultations, as they view it as an inability to take the proper decision to take. They can therefore easily integrate into zones of conflict where they could be able to demonstrate their authority, especially in situations of emergency.

Upper zone writers with light pressure are in fact the most people inclined group of individuals They have the ability to make thoughtful attention to the feelings and opinions of others as opposed to the writers with heavy pressure who effortlessly take action with little thought. The lighter pressure writers in the upper zone are more tolerant of the restrictions of others, while more sacrifices for others are made by those in those in the light pressure category.

The attributes displayed by lighter pressure writers allows them to easily fit into the hospitality industry and service-related industry due to their person-centered style of living.

Lower zone

Lower zone writers are divided in straight stroke and loop writers. Straight lower zone writers are more likely to employ this style, which indicates their eagerness to finish their work. The completion of a project is their top priority, there is no necessity to be careful about the activities they are involved in.

Loop writers exhibit their necessity to be more precise by displaying a lot of enthusiasm in the work they're preparing to do. They are more in the creative set of writers when compared with straight line writers in the lower zone. Loop writers are more patient as opposed to those who write straight lines. Loop writers tend to be more focused on an activity that requires constant effort like wood carving, or other art tasks that yield the greatest results dependent on the amount of effort required in the task.

SIZE

In general, people are recognized for their size of writing but some may have a greater and smaller. The handwriting size can be divided into three distinct layers, which are: Large small, middle and large.

Large size

The larger size, which typically falls within the 9mm range and over is typically related to those who are more outgoing. This characteristic is linked to the cheerful personality of those that are quick to start conversations and are often emotional. They are easily able to fit into interactions that require constant contact with people since they are able to be extremely friendly and also ebullient.

The writers in this group would work well in jobs like teaching, television broadcasting, and various other roles that could make their expressive capabilities excellent tool for communicating.

Middle size

Middle size writers are often associated with those who have traits that are in between the larger and smaller size writers. Middle size writers are able to effortlessly control their emotions when they are required to either being expressive or reserved. Middle-sized writers are better in control emotionally compared to their larger size counterparts.

Small size

This group of writers is highly analytical and calculative. They are the thinkers of the three sizes of writers. They're not as emotional as the larger-sized writers and could be able to fit into specific positions that require analytical abilities. Job descriptions that require a an intense concentration level prove to be useful for those in this group. Jobs that require high amounts of computing and surgical procedures that require a precise precision could be beneficial for this group of people.

Small-sized writers aren't fast at initiating communication They also display an excessive humor during interactions with people. Their reluctance at issues of concern to them is evident when they are in a situation that is provoking.

They are nevertheless strong in their academics and the capacity to concentrate on specific goals and work the achievement of which they wish to accomplish. They're not easily distracted by the surroundings as could be for writers of large size They are however great at engaging in a way that is without the interference of large numbers of people.

Line SPACING

Line spacing plays an important role in the study of a handwriting. Different people have different degrees of spacing between lines , as can be easily determined by writing with a plane. A plane paper can be an excellent source for knowing the personality of an individual, along with other traits that can be identified by the writing style of an individual.

We offer 'wide line spacing' and closed line spacing between lines, as explained below.

Wide line-spacing

When lines are spread out people prefer staying away from the scene in particular when it demands the commitment of some kind to the course or project. These individuals do not totally commit to what is agreed upon, since they exhibit the signs of being resistant to an undertaking.

In addition, it is said that a lack of understanding about an issue could lead individuals to use large spacing, particularly in cases where it isn't an usual characteristic of one. It is apparent by students in an exam and students with a poor comprehension regarding the question(s) given are likely to use wide space in their answer books due to the fact that it is easy to comprehend. In addition to the necessity to fill answer books quickly to impress their teachers, with little content the students lack the desire of the brain to write down the contents on paper. This will reflect on the spacing of their answer booklets.

Furthermore, when someone is under pressure while making statements, the spacing of her lines will likely to be larger than she intended due to the fact that this mental distaste is transmitted on to the hand by nerve signals. This kind of analysis is extremely effective in carrying out investigations of criminal cases, and for making the to sign a contract. As law enforcement personnel who have a good understanding of graphology, they will be able make better judgments while doing their job.

Line-spacing with a closed line

The style of writing is a sign of the action-oriented, one who is willing to participate in whatever is required to be accomplished. The surge of energy that comes generated by the brain is evident in the speed with that an individual is willing to take on the task, and without the need for space that could be an unnecessary use of time or resources.

Additionally, students who have a an understanding of the questions they are asked are quick to respond quickly that is evident by how fast their hand movements which requires no thought or delay. In addition, as this students have a vast in their knowledge of the subject they will be tested on and are aiming to reduce the space on paper by limiting the spaces between lines. This is a fascinating way to identify the key aspects of the students' testing process.

Page AREA

Page margins include the left top, right, and bottom margins analysis. The margins of the pages have something to say about the persona of an individual as described in the following sections;

Top margin

A person who wants to start his writing in the topmost area of the page indicates the desire to reach goals and goals. They are able to show a great attitude while taking on challenges because of their dynamism. The challenge of a task is a source of pride to these people They do not linger in their approach to a strategy. Indecisiveness isn't a feature of their behaviour, however they are able to move in the quickest time possible.

Bottom margin

Bottom margins reflect the practicality of their writing as well as their the ability to work. Bottom margin writers can put a concentrated effort into whatever they want to do. Their strength is due to their endurance. They aren't only open to new challenges as the feeling of not having achieved achievement is likely to keep them from doing it. Being involved in an odd job is typical of the group They may take on a job which is outside of the current norm of doing things. The more different from the norm they operate the more fascinating they find themselves.

Left margin

Writers who are close to the left margin indicate that they live close to families and have a strong root. A desire to be influence over their close family members and family is important to them. Engagement that takes away from their roots isn't appealing to them.

Right margin

Writers from the right margin are worried regarding the future, and what lies ahead. They are futurists who want to start thinking about the possibilities that lie ahead. Right margin writers aren't dissatisfied with the present, they are looking for the future. reaching out to others is also considered to be something they have Their minds aren't focused on themselves but is open and a display of an attitude of apathy. Awareness of the requirements of others is an attribute of this group of people.

Engaging in charitable causes would benefit right margin writers. Their caring for others could be beneficial in the healthcare industry and the hospitality sector. This type of analysis can be beneficial in recommending career choices as well as other areas of self-development.

WORD SPACING

Word spacing is classified by narrow spacing and wide spacing.

Wide space is a symbol of those who are genuinely conscious of their space and do not constantly seek of a companionship with other people. Like the phlegmatic personality group of people tend to be extremely valuable to their private lives. They might be ideal for work that requires only interactions with others, since they appreciate the importance of personal focus in whatever it is they are engaged in.

The wide spacing can also be a significative of people who are quiet and not too sociable. This characteristic is beneficial in a relationship that is not demanding of people's on the relationship side.

Narrow spacing

This typically indicates the attitude of writers who are extremely lusty for company with other people. The similarities between their personalities are of the optimistic people, and they exhibit their communication abilities when with others. They are more perceptive than their broader-spread counterparts. They exhibit more friendship and aren't silent aggressors. However, they are able to effortlessly express their thoughts about any negative or positive treatment. They are also inclined to share their possessions with other people. This type of person is more charitable than others, as they can easily share their space like they are able to share their possessions.

Since they are typically more expressive, this group of people would perform very well in interactions that require a significant amount of interaction with others as well as.

THREAD

The writers in this group make up their writings in an edging pattern. They demonstrate one of the artistic signals in the various patterns of writing. They also are extremely considerate of their work and do not plan to spend more than is necessary on any particular job and are conscious of the need not to waste time and resources. The thread-like quality in their work is intriguing to those who regard these people to be well-educated and mentally healthy.

Despite that, they possess the capacity to impress other people with their substance, something they aren't actually.

WAVYLINE

This is a sign of adaptability and the ability to think on their feet. They exhibit a high degree of creativity and their capacity to innovate whenever the need arises. They are extremely worried about the aesthetic aspect of any task they decide to complete. They are able to contribute to inventive projects and innovations. Engineering can be a good location to develop their capabilities. They are also creative in nature and may be extremely efficient. However, they should not overlook the possibility that some people employ their skills to deceive, if proper the proper care is not taken when dealing with them.

Writing and our BEHAVOUR

Thus, we can see the connection between a person's handwriting and their personality give them an advantage when deciding on potential acquaintances or business partners. In addition, with the growing demands for soft skills there's no better time to get a head start in graphology than today.

Many people who had unaware of graphology, take an interested in it and start to look up more information regarding the way they write. This is accompanied by the constant request from me to provide them with additional details about this topic, in addition to any other new information that could be apparent in my analysis of their handwriting when they mail me. (N/B Note: Go to the end of this book to find a website and contact details for examination of your handwriting). Once you've become acquainted with the requirements for conducting a thorough analysis of your handwriting then you'll be more confident when making decisions about an crucial partnership or involvement to join.

HAPPNESS INDEX

Do we really connect the handwriting of a person to their happiness index? The happiness index reveals the level of happiness an individual can be over a length of time. Certain scholars have found a connection between the genetic characteristics of an individual and his or his happiness index. Many regarded genetic makeup as an important factor in determining around 40 percent of a person's overall wellbeing which indicates the significant amount of impact that the genetic characteristics of an individual can affect the attitude or outlook of a person.

It is also possible to determine that a particular family could exhibit a greater degree of happiness when compared with neighbors who are more fortunate in other aspects of their lives opposed to the family with the highest happiness. This is a sign of the role that genetics and personality play.

It's also been observed by some research experts that one's environment plays a significant impact on the development and personality traits of a person, and because we can connect the personality of a person to his writing style, we can establish a link between the environment one lives in and his writing style.

The method of communicating or interfacing with one's peers is a way to get an accurate idea of the place of residence of an person. For instance, there's an area in Nigeria called Warri, in which the majority of residents are believed to be confident and sociable. This is a good example of the role that the surroundings of the individual has on their personality. This is why we can identify the connection that connects the environment to the persona and finally to the writing style.

This makes it clear that there could be distinct characteristics among those who live in the same area in particular if they share the similar personalities.

RACIAL INFLUENCE

If the environment around the individual plays a part in the style of writing of an individual then the racial class of an individual will play a part to contribute to handwriting. Certain people believe that Black Americans to have a personality that is overly expressive, and that trait could be evident in the writing style of a writer that is associated with writing styles such as narrow word spacing, big dimensions and a slant which are a sign of expressive individuals.

This influence from race can prove useful in situations where it is necessary to the identity of the author of the particular note or text. So, a graphologist is capable of identifying similarities in the style of writing with an assortment of individuals who are closely connected in some way or other. This type of analysis helps identify collaborators for a specific task or activity.

Life Expectations Through Handwriting

Some researchers came to conclusions which linked the happiness score of people with their life expectation. This result, which is not completely accepted by all, suggests that those with more happiness levels tend to be healthier than people who are unhappy or unhappy than their happier peers.

Many factors are believed to influence the happy state of a person, these elements include a feeling of belonging to an organized and healthy group, in addition to other things. The possibility of being a part of a healthy group is evident through the study of the individual's handwriting.

In addition If the correlation with happiness index and lifespan remains to be true, we could determine the connection between life expectancy and handwriting of a person. Thus we can identify the pattern of writing that reflects the most happy person.

Additionally, if the handwriting of a person is affected by their personality according to the text, and we are of the opinion that the character of an individual is made up of her genetic makeup then it is also possible to say that genetic makeup can have a major influence on the life span of individuals.

If you are able to recall the results of a study done a few years in the past, regarding how life expectancy relates to as well as racial diversity? It was discovered that an Japanese group was found to have the highest life expectancies on earth. This adds further proof regarding the relation between life expectancy and the genetic makeup of the environment that have an impact on the writing style of an individual.

AFFECTIVE EXPRESSION AND WRITING PATTERN

The book also attempts to discover the connection between your handwriting and the facial expression of a person. The writing of an individual can give valuable information about the facial expressions of the person. Knowing the handwriting of an individual could help in determining the humour displayed through the body language of the individual or how they express themselves. It is important to note how emotional a person is, the higher the likelihood that there will be a constant shift in the expression of an individual.

The graphology knowledge can aid in making the right decisions for those who are working in jobs that require certain characteristics as well as facial expressions. For instance job descriptions that require employees to maintain the expressions of a smile that signal friendlyness could be achieved by a thorough understanding of the analysis of handwriting.

Certain job descriptions might have employees wearing an unfriendly expression on their face such as those seen in employees of security or protection service This characteristic can be identified by the style of writing of those who exhibit these characteristics. A hostile expression of the face is more common among those who don't want to be in others' company who do not need being in the spotlight. This is similar to what has been previously mentioned with regard to broad word spacing writers who display the desire for their own space. They may show this in their facial expressions.

People who have a more expressive personalities as evident by their writing style are more open and constantly seeking being with other people.

The importance of GRAPHOLOGY

The significance of graphology can't be overemphasized. Constant attention is paid to the ways it can be used to improve the working state of our society. The use of graphology is utilized by law enforcement personnel who rely on graphologists to conduct forensic analysis of death threats and other documents that are written from anonymous criminals. Other uses of graphology will be described below.

COUSELLING

Counsellors can use the information clients' handwriting provides as extremely helpful in handling situations, since the personalities of the client plays a crucial part during counselling sessions. Counsellors can handle issues more efficiently with the benefit of knowing graphology. The anger display previously mentioned can be easily played out in the writing style of a person particularly when the handwriting differs from what the individual is used to and therefore the understanding of this change in the style of writing of a customer can assist counsellors better handle these situations, which require the management of anger and an expression of compassion.

TEAM BUILDING

Individuals who are more active might indicate those who make more effective team players. People who are proactive aren't usually indecisive, but they are more likely to have more expressive personalities, despite the tendency to be indecisive. Therefore, a handwriting analyst might be a good choice to build a team when there is a need for. The ideal mix of a successful team requires people who are both active and expressive, along with people who are concentrated and focused on the task to be managed. So, the ability to identify these characteristics or characteristics based on the handwriting of the team members expected to be a part of it could be beneficial to build a team and team selection.

THE CHOICE OF COMPANIONSHIP

The personalities of individuals vary greatly, with some people proving to be more social opposed to other people, and others prefer to have small interactions in the presence of their fellow humans and so whatever selecting the best partner requires a thorough understanding of what your friend's needs and having that in mind can help you make the best choice on who you want to be a friend. Since the handwriting of an individual gives sufficient information regarding the personality or temperament of the person, like some marriage counselors recommend marriage choices by the personality of an individual, you can also choose your partner by analyzing your own personal interpretation of the handwriting.

RECRUITING

As mentioned earlier about the process of selecting candidates in the case of candidates who submit documents or applications that are handwritten expert handwriting plays a part in the selection process particularly for high-paying or sought-after jobs. Therefore, having a basic understanding of this and a better understanding of the characteristics successful candidates must possess can be advantageous to those who have some understanding of graphology. Because the job market that require management positions of a high-level will require recruiters to find applicants who aren't just technically competent, but that are also well-versed in the area of emotional intelligence. There is a growing demand for people who are emotionally intelligent and are thought to have the skills required to succeed in higher levels of management is a signal for recruiters to search for such qualities that can be identified in the writing of people like the ones mentioned earlier.

Career Planning

There are jobs that require a significant amount in interaction with service suppliers and their customers. These jobs require employees who are sensitive and empathetic and also creative in the way they communicate services. The understanding of the style of writing that best meets these requirements can be useful when making decisions regarding career choices and the development of career. Writers who wrote about temperament have also made use of this advice regarding personality traits and the path to a career for each person. Since the character of an individual is determined by her handwriting your career choices can be derived from handwriting.

AFFECTATION PRESENT AND FUTURE of GRAPHOLOGY

There is no limit to graphology's potential application in the future as it is currently used to forensic applications of signatures even if it is signed using digital devices or screens. In addition, forgery can be being detected today through the examination of the emotional state of fraudsters whenever they sign documents, as opposed to when they are honest or in a good mental state.

Additionally, the study of graphology could be helpful in determining the character of a person and also the level of their emotional intelligence. If the person's handwriting provides a clue about the degree of emotional intelligence It is likely that employers will find this appealing when they are looking for workers. and recruitment agencies will consider it helpful when looking for the ideal candidate for certain roles, so it shouldn't be a surprise to find a company that asks job applicants to sign their letters in hand in the age of digital like it is for certain. These requirements could be due to the requirement to identify candidates that are more expressive or less or require a lot of concentration, but little human interaction could favor applicants who are not as than expressive, however they are more analytical, as their handwriting might show. However, jobs which require excellent customer relations might be more suited to candidates who are more expressive and emotional similar to the way their handwriting reflects.

Furthermore, certain traits are expected of those who are in the top positions of management in top firms. The criteria used by the recruitment agencies aren't limited to technical or hard skills. The reason for this is that the recruiters are aware that top performers require more than just technical skills to be successful within Fortune 500 companies. Diverse levels of proficiency are considered for those who are in continuous interaction with board members, and an excellent level of interaction with staff members and top-quality customers. Business partnerships is influenced or modified through the study of the writing of the prospective business partner. By knowing the character of a person it is easy to know whether every business idea held by a person is published in the past or is not spoken, which is what experienced business partners will prefer to see more to gain, especially in a pitching for business, or sponsorship pitch.

MAKER OF AN OPTIMIST OR PESSIMIST

The outlook to be an optimist pessimist is evident by her writing style, people who are both generally have different views on the outcome of a situation and could provide clues to their personality from their handwriting. The optimist is more like writers who compose on the right-hand edge of the margin which indicates a passion and hope for something positive in the near future.

The pessimist on the contrary side is more cautious when undertaking a task with a uncertain result. These traits could help you in your own analysis of someone that is most likely be an optimist. So, the knowledge you have gained can assist you in identifying some aspects easily.

The people who are most likely to be unperturbed by challenges

The person who is optimistic is less likely to be influenced by events The quality of this characteristic can be assessed by the writing style of an individual. The person who is optimistic can quickly forget things that bother them, and this is essential to move forward or engage in a new endeavor. So, identifying such individuals through their handwriting can help in making choices for those with greater capacity to endure.

SHORT TERM AND LONG-TERM INVESTMENT

Let's look at the connection that the writing of an individual is able to show towards their desire for short-term or long-term pleasure. People who are seeking pleasure in the short term want to enjoy the pleasures of their life right now without thinking about what's to come. This group of people tends toward people who have more emotion and expression with little time for analytical thinking.

Analytical thinkers will think about what's ahead by weighing the pros and cons of satisfying their immediate desires to the expense of future gains. Handwriting of a person can be used to distinguish people who are analytical against those worried about the current situation current. We can conclude that the writing of an individual can be used to distinguish between short-term pleasure seekers and long-term pleasure seeking.

In accordance with the description of people who are analytical and emotional it is possible to say those who are seeking pleasure in the short-term are associated with right slant writers whereas long-term pleasure seekers are associated with left-slant writers. The analytical skills that is displayed by long-term pleasure seekers is apparent in their writing patterns which indicates the need to meet established goals and reach goals in the future, as is typical of left margin authors.

The information gained from these groups of people can be useful when deciding on the appropriate action to take in a particular situation in view of the possibility that the short-term pleasure seeker is likely to offer suggestions to meet the current demand at that time, while the long term pleasure seeker could offer suggestions that could provide long-term benefit with no immediate gain as a primary factor.

AFFECTING MARRIAGE CHOICE AND HANDWRITING RELATIONSHIP

Certain authors have suggested a connection between our personalities and the necessity of making the best decision about an affluent or wealthy spouse according to the personality of the one who one plans to marry. The majority of these authors advise that there must be a blend of the character that of the male and the woman, and suggest that the two personalities should be in harmony. For instance when a man is more of an analytical nature and perhaps a lack of expressiveness He should match his personality by selecting an empathetic wife to be more emotional and expressive and able to create the best relationship.

If the idea given above is correct and we've established previously that the character of a person can be determined by the handwriting of a person so we could also say that the choice of the best life partner can be based on the handwriting of the people taking into consideration.

In the main the concept of having partners with complementary characteristics as suggested by some researchers means having these combinations written in the handwriting of the couples who are planning to marry;

* A writer with a right slant and left slant writers

* High pressure author, and one with a lighter pressure

* Big size writers as well as small-sized writers.

* Spacers with narrow words as well as one with a broad word spacer

* A top margin author, and an author with a bottom margin

However, the most effective decision to marry is made by the individual who is involved through his faith in God to guide him in making the right choice. Therefore, there is no reason to consider these assertions as a law. The elements that decide the viability of a marriage is not only based on the signature of an intended partner, but this type of contribution solely serves to provide an indication of the character of the other party particularly when a person lives in a remote region with no personal contacts, yet having the privilege of composing letters.

Chapter 11: Lies

Everybody lies It's the unfortunate truth. Human nature is a fact.

In some situations such as an interview, for instance it is essential to establish if the candidate is genuine or is lying!

There are some methods that analyze handwriting can help you identify a fraudster and stop you from falling for fraud.

Speed

Apart from the strokes that a person's handwriting, speed also is something that warrants your focus. Be aware if someone appears to be a bit slow in writing. This could mean either impaired mental capacity or lack of sincerity. If you don't think the person you're speaking to has a mental handicap or in some way then there is more than average probability that they are lying.

Normal adults will write in a normal pace particularly when there isn't any real reason to be so conscious in the selection of words. A slow handwriting could indicate that someone is conscious of hiding the truth about something.

Wide Gaps Between Words and Print Letters

Wide spaces between words could indicate that the person is lying, specifically regarding what they wrote. For instance, if you wrote "I am honest and sincere person who doesn't like to be lied to" in this manner you can be sure that they're not the words they wrote.

The absence of printed letters could also be a sign of deceit or secrecy. But, this doesn't necessarily mean that the person writing it is lying. It could just be an indication of a shady personality generally.

"Cover" Words and Stroke Words

A cover stroke occurs where the last stroke of the last letter of an expression is positioned over a small portion of or the entire word (or the entire word). The stroke that is the last "covers" other letters and is the reason for the term "cover stroke".

This is an indication of defensiveness. People tend to be defensive when they have something to hide.

"Felon's Claw" In Letters

"Felon's Claw" or "felon's claw" occurs when someone makes the shape of a claw after an down stroke, like"g" or "y," the latter being lowercase "g" or "y" such as. The "claw" is formed somewhat similar to an upside-down "U".

In graphology, this is usually associated with bitterness, guilt, and bad impulses. It is usually associated with criminal conduct which is why it's called "felon's claw". The more specific the meaning of the claw the greater frequently the author displays these characteristics and the more aware of his guilt.

Normal Script Vs. Signature

There is a significant distinction between the handwriting of the form of a paragraph or text, and their signature can be a sign of duplicity. They might display a public appearance which is different from their behavior in private. Although they might appear pretentious and arrogant, they might not be exhibiting an act of criminality.

O's and A's

The properties of lowercase a's and o's could assist in identifying the most dangerous type of liar: the pathological lying. If the lowercase letters of A's and O's have two huge inner loops with one loop on the left and one on the right side, there's a good chance that they are an obnoxious lying.

Be cautious when dealing when dealing with authors of this kind and take everything they write with the grain of salt.

These are some indicators to look out for when assessing the honesty of a person. If an individual displays one of these characteristics, or multiple of them, it's wise to verify the claims they make about their truth before you grant the person your trust.

Chapter 12: Sexuality And Compatibility

Three zones for handwriting three zones of handwriting: the upper zone middle zone, as well as the lower zone.

The higher zone is concerned with the mind, the middle zone is focused on aspects of life in general while the lower zone is where you can see the physical motivations of an individual.

This chapter we'll discuss the lower zone. It is the part of handwriting which make up the lower loops of letters, like the lower loops that make up the alphabets "y", "g" or "j".

The lower area is the physical dimensions of the person. Undoubtedly, one of the most powerful, primal yet the most intricate of human physical desires is the sexual urge. Because of this, the lower zone is often utilized to study the sexual preferences of an individual.

You may be wondering whether it is possible to get a better understanding of the sex drives of a person through a glance at their handwriting? It's an absolute yes. In the end, the person's sexual inclination is just a part of the personality. And as in the previous chapter you can gain plenty of details about personality by studying handwriting.

The most important points to concentrate on when analyzing sexual assault is the loops that are lower in the letter "y", "g" and "j". When you look at these loops you will be able to get an idea about the amount of the sexual intimacy a person requires and how often the need to meet these needs and the level of sexual resentment that he/she experiences.

Long, moderately wide loops With heavy Tracing

This could be a sign of an sex-driven desire that is extremely strong. It could be for physical pleasure or even that there are emotions involved. The amount of emphasis the writer attaches to sexual pleasure is indicated by the width of the loop.

Since people who have this kind of handwriting are characterized by strong sexual desires, they need lots of sex in order to be satisfied and also an abundance of imagination and diversity. They are not averse to boredom, so they're willing to engage in lots of experimentation and creativity.

Small or shortened loops that have Light Tracing

People with this kind of handwriting don't take part in lots of sexual sport generally. The physical and emotional exertion is too for their style of writing. That's why they usually appear to be uninterested in sexual relations. It's not because they are not interested in their partners in love. The issue is that the physical strain needed discourages them from frequent intimate contact.

Incomplete Loops

It could be an indication of sexual discontent particularly if the person previously used loops that were complete in their script. Someone who composes in this manner could feel that they are having little or any sexual intimacy, or may feel dissatisfied with his partner. It could also be a sign of a sexual trauma of a different kind.

Normal, controlled loops that aren't Excessively Long or wide

The key to success is moderation for writers of this type. They possess a moderate sexual urge that lets them focus their energy and physical effort on other pursuits in addition. They can control their sexual activity to the extent to ensure that sexual activity is not required to be a consistent cycle to feel sexually satisfied. It could happen as frequently as once or two weeks, or as frequently as several times throughout the day.

Very Long, Inflated Loops, Wide

It's wise to be cautious of sexual partners who write this type of writing. People with this style tend over exaggerating their sexual abilities. They are known to boast about their accomplishments and exploits, however, when the time comes for them to reveal what they have achieved they don't appear to be able to live up to their pride.

The exaggerated loops symbolize the excessive fantasy that drains the person of the motivation to succeed. Because they feel uneasy about themselves, they are also prone to look for numerous partners to boost confidence in themselves.

Here are some tips to help you identify specific aspects of a person's sexual drive from their manner of writing. But don't be too eager to make assumptions from these signs alone. To fully comprehend the character of a person's personality the person, an extensive examination of all handwriting must be done. These handwriting patterns can be excellent indicators, however they're not the only way to know.

Sexual attraction isn't the only factor in relationships worth examining. If you're considering an investigation of a possible partner's handwriting, compatibility is another element to find out.

How can you tell the compatibility?

The easiest method to determine this is to determine how similar the handwriting of your partner is in comparison to your own. There is evidence that shows couples who have lived together happily for a lengthy period tend to have the same handwriting.

The reason is actually very simple. If handwriting is a sign of character, it follows that those with similar handwriting also have similar personality traits. Studies on relationships show that those who share interests and share more things than one thing in common be successful in their relationships in contrast to the traditional cliché that "opposites draw".

But don't be discouraged if you and your partner's handwriting don't coincide! Certain people are in a relationship because they "complete" each the other. Couples such as this complement each to each other and offset each other's weaknesses by leveraging their strengths.

Chapter 13: Handwriting Analysis

In the first grade in primary school, you were taught how to write in the same manner like everyone else. The teacher showed you pictures that illustrated the alphabets A B, C and so on and you copied the illustrations and then learned them. Similar is the case to your peers. They were all presented with the same pictures of the alphabet by your teacher.

But, even so did you notice that nobody in your class has exactly similar handwriting? Did you ever think about why even after the same lessons in writing as well as the writing books and teachers nobody ever ends with the same handwriting?

In reality, as you got older, you may have noticed the distinct different handwriting styles of your friends. It was probably your mother who put that note on your refrigerator. You can tell from the note that was rolled up and handed to you during class came from your most beloved friend.

Utilizing this distinctness in handwriting to determine the traits of individuals is the basis of analysis of handwriting.

The art that studies handwriting patterns, which is also referred to in graphology has an extensive time. It was popularized in France in the 1600's where monks and theologians chose to make the subject their main focus. Europe can be considered to be the origin of this field. Even famous philosophers, like Goethe and Lavater believed the fact that writing can aid in the derivation of character and personality.

In the 1930s the handwriting analysis gained prominence within America. United States. A penmanship teacher observed that, despite the uniformity of his teaching methods and instructing pupils in small groups, the handwriting was unique that was evident in their strokes. They had their "mark" according to the way he described it. He made meticulous observations and made use of the known knowledge, and ultimately had significant contributions to the field as well as gaining popularity in US.

Years of research have steadily transformed handwriting analysis into the rigorous discipline that it is nowadays. Today, it is widely employed as a preliminary evaluation method for hiring and employee advancement. Handwriting is an instrument to determine a person's capability to cope under pressure, perform as part of a team, and resolve issues. It can also be utilized in criminal investigation.

But the benefits of handwriting analysis isn't restricted to these specific areas. Personally you can utilize it to gain more understanding of yourself as well as your family members and friends. You'll be amazed by the depth of information that a few words written by hand can provide.

To witness the outcomes of your own handwriting analysis Here is a great practice to do before continuing with this book:

Write the sentence in your handwriting of choice at least five times, observing the structure of paragraphs: "The quick brown fox leaps across the dog who is lazy". This sentence incorporates all letters in the alphabet . It is referred to as pangram. This will give you a full and complete review of the handwriting you have. If you wish to create a second paragraph about things you'd like to talk about. More you compose, more precise an analysis of your findings will appear.

Additionally, if you use several styles that you write in (such as a distinct print script and cursive script) make sure you do the same exercise for both. However, any interpretations that differ that are based on the style you employ most often should be given higher weight in the analysis.

Conclusion

Congrats on reaching the conclusion to this book

But don't be dismayed if you are confused. It takes a lot time to get the perfect handwriting analysis.

Experts usually need years to gain enough experience to be able to recognize the persona of a handwriting even then, it's not something that is accomplished with a single glance.

This book is merely one of the first steps into the fascinating and complicated realm of analysis and handwriting. They are a great way to go in helping you expand your knowledge and sharpen your skills.

Handwriting analysis is an incredibly useful instrument. But do not make the error of thinking that you can have all the information about a person using this method on your own. Human beings are complex and countless years of research have yet to discover the secrets of our minds.

Be aware that any kind of analysis of the personality isn't completely accurate. Even the most rigid sciences have their own uncertainties The same could be said about the art of graphology.

This book will give you the ability to comprehend your own and other people better. Make use of this knowledge with a sense of responsibility and control.
All the best!